Small Business Accounting

USER GUIDE

Welcome to QuickBooks

This user guide is designed to help you get the most out of the features that QuickBooks has to offer. This guide also provides some business concepts to help you better understand some of the accounting concepts used in QuickBooks.

What's in this Guide?

QuickBooks Keyboard Shortcuts 52

Quick Exercises 53

New To QuickBooks

Begin By Creating Your Company File

A QuickBooks company file contains all the financial records for your business. It's easy to create using the Setup window, which appears automatically after you launch QuickBooks.

You can also reach this window from the menu by choosing **File > New Company**.

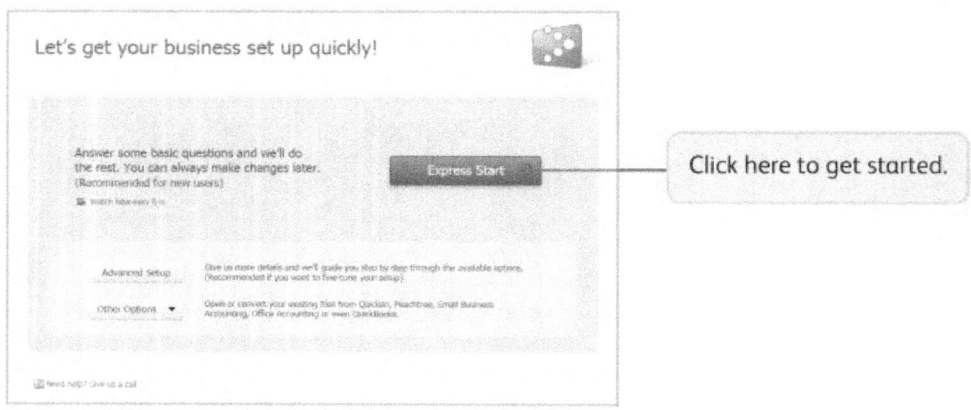

Next, Add Your Business Info

After you create your company file, add your business info: the people you do business with, your bank accounts, and your products or services. No data to enter or import right now? No problem! You can add it as you work in QuickBooks.

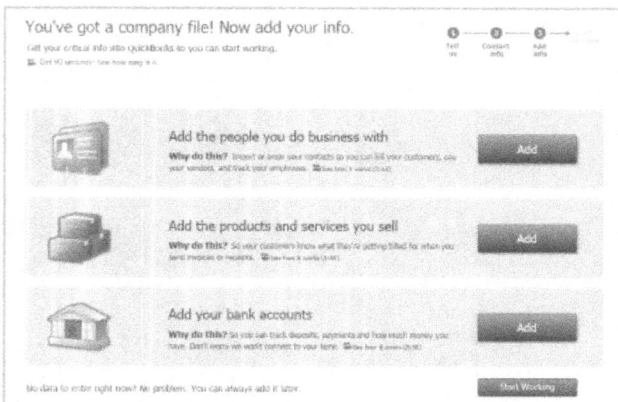

To come back to this window later, go to the Help menu and choose **Quick Start Center**, then click **Return to Add Info**.

Decisions to Make Before You Start

This chapter will help you to make choices as you set up your company and will suggest things you should do after completing your setup.

Who owns your business?

First, determine how your business is owned. Is it a sole proprietorship, a partnership, or a corporation? The differences include the tax form you file, your income tax filing deadlines, and how your profits are apportioned.

What accounting method should I use?

There are two common methods of bookkeeping: cash and accrual. Your method determines how you report income and expenses on your tax forms. When you begin your business, you need to decide which bookkeeping method to use. *Check with your accountant before you make your choice.*

It's best not to switch to a different accounting system after you've selected one. However, you can switch between cash and accrual reports in QuickBooks at any time, without affecting your accounting records. By default, QuickBooks creates reports on an accrual basis.

What accounting do I need to know?

Using QuickBooks requires very little accounting knowledge. You need to understand a chart of accounts and the different types of accounts on it. You don't have to know about debits and credit, journal entries, or closing periods. Your QuickBooks chart of accounts can have:

- Balance sheet accounts
- Income accounts
- Expense accounts
- Cost of goods sold accounts
- Non-posting accounts (which don't appear on your balance sheet)

Some of these accounts are created for you automatically. For example, the first time you create an invoice or statement charge, QuickBooks automatically creates an accounts receivable (A/R) account. You'll add other accounts, such as your

---

checking account, during setup using the EasyStep Interview. You can create and modify your accounts as needed at any time.

Should I Track Customers?

Some businesses don't need to keep track of the names of customers. An example is a retail store or service business that always receives payment with the sale or service.

However, here are some situations in which you would want to track customer names:

- Customers receive your goods or services and then pay you later.
- Customers are supposed to pay a regular monthly fee, and you want to track who has paid and who hasn't.
- You want to track income (and perhaps expenses as well) by customer.

Why You Probably Need To Set Up Items?

In QuickBooks, both kinds of businesses—service and product—can benefit by setting up items to track the services they provide or the products they sell to customers.

Note: In QuickBooks, "sales" is a broad term. It refers to any business action that generates income in exchange for services or products, even if you don't think of what you do as selling. For example, a psychologist with patients, a graphic designer with clients, and a roofing contractor with customers all would set up items in QuickBooks for what they sell.

Setting-Up Items

You can add items at any time—as part of setting up QuickBooks or whenever you think of an item you need to use.

Remember, items are for the services or items you buy and sell. You also may need special calculating items that calculate subtotals and discounts, and that apply specific sales tax rates.

Working with Items

After you have set up items, use them to enter estimates, sales, purchase orders, sales orders, actual purchases, and disposition of fixed assets. Remember, QuickBooks uses the term sales broadly; it can mean the performance of services or the assessment of fees as well as the sale of products.

Things to Think about after You're Finished

Create Reports to Check Your Setup

After you've finished setting up your company in QuickBooks and making any adjustments, create reports to check that QuickBooks has the right numbers. Both reports should show the same balances for your accounts.

Maintain Your Previous Accounting System

If your business existed before you began to use QuickBooks, make sure you keep your previous accounting system complete.

Connect QuickBooks to the Internet

Your PC must be connected to the Internet through an Internet Service Provider (ISP). Your work PC may be connected through a local area network (LAN). If you can read e-mail or browse the Web, you are connected to the Internet.

You don't need Internet access to use QuickBooks, but the ability to "go online" can easily double the power and flexibility of your software. It allows you to take advantage of Internet-only features in QuickBooks.
Consider these additional possibilities:

1. **Explore opportunities with QuickBooks' connected services**
From the Company menu, select Business Services Navigator.
2. **Receive QuickBooks updates**
Download and install QuickBooks software updates as they become available.
3. **Download tax table information**
If you've signed up for the QuickBooks Payroll, you can download the latest tax tables.

To Set Up An Internet Connection:

QuickBooks automatically launches the Internet Connection Setup wizard if you have not used QuickBooks on your computer before. If you're already using QB then follow these steps:

1- From the Help menu, choose Internet Connection Setup.
2- Follow the onscreen instructions. Click Next to move through the screens. If you need help at any time, click Help.
3- Click Done.

Update QuickBooks to the Latest Release

From time to time, Intuit provides updates to QuickBooks. There are several ways to update your version of QuickBooks:

▪ **Automatic Update:** This option prompts you when a new release is available for your version of QuickBooks. If you choose to update when prompted, QuickBooks down-loads the necessary files to your computer via the Internet in the background, with little impact on your computer's performance.
▪ **Manual Download:** With this method, you decide when to download an update via the Internet to your computer. You can use this method at any time—even if your computer is set up to download updates automatically.
▪ **From www.quickbooks.ca/:** Visit our Web site to download the latest release.
▪ **Multiuser Update:** When updating multiple users, the new update is downloaded via the Internet to a local server for each user to then download to their computer.

Using the Home page to move around in QuickBooks

The Home page gives you a big picture of how your business tasks fit together. It opens automatically whenever you open a company file.

You can do all your tasks just using the menus. The menus contain the same tasks as the Home page, and more.

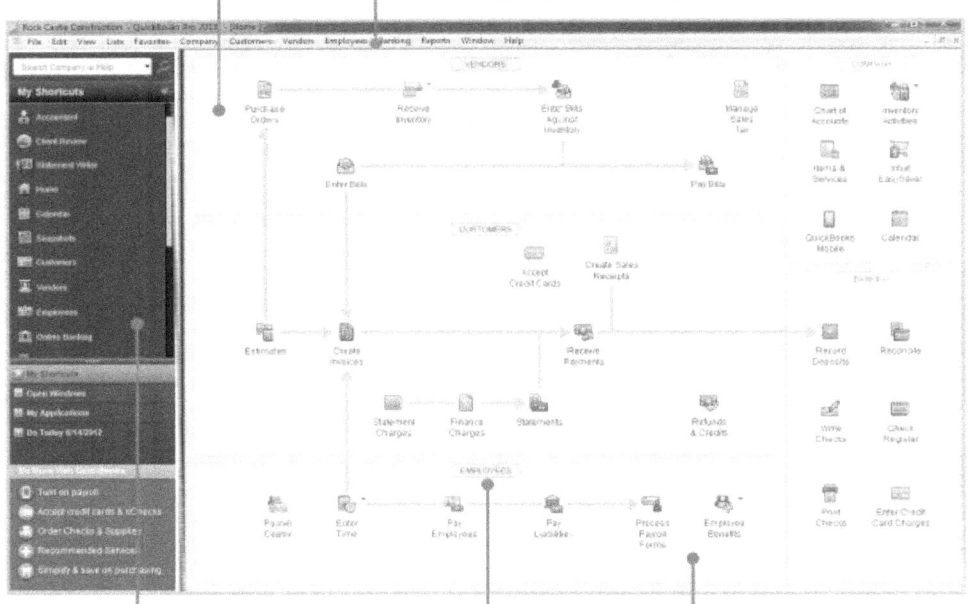

The Icon Bar includes shortcuts to many parts of QuickBooks. To create your own shortcuts, click **Customize Shortcuts**.

To customize the Home page, choose **Edit > Preferences > Desktop View**, and then click the **Company Preferences** tab.

You go directly to the centers by clicking on these icons.

Using Centers

There are 3 main QuickBooks Centers, one each for customers, vendors, and employees. Use the centers to manage and view all of your customer, vendor, and employee information and transactions, without having to sift through multiple windows.

All of these centers work the same way. We'll use the Customer Center to show you how they work.

All of your customers show up here.

Click here to see all of your customer transactions.

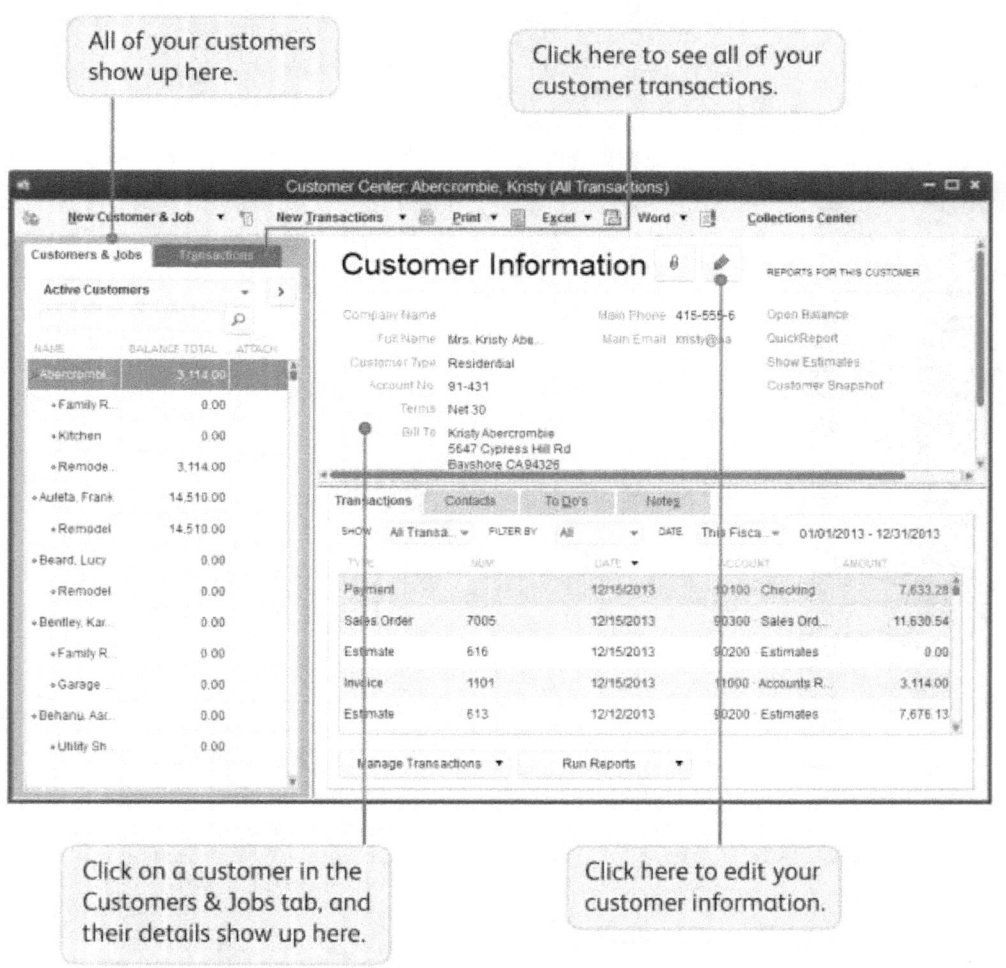

Click on a customer in the Customers & Jobs tab, and their details show up here.

Click here to edit your customer information.

Using Forms

All of your everyday QuickBooks tasks, like invoicing, paying bills, and writing checks, are done on forms. You can reach every form in QuickBooks from the Home page or the menus. We'll use an invoice to show you how forms work.

Use the arrows to move through a list of transactions.

Click the tabs on this ribbon to find everything you need to do on a form.

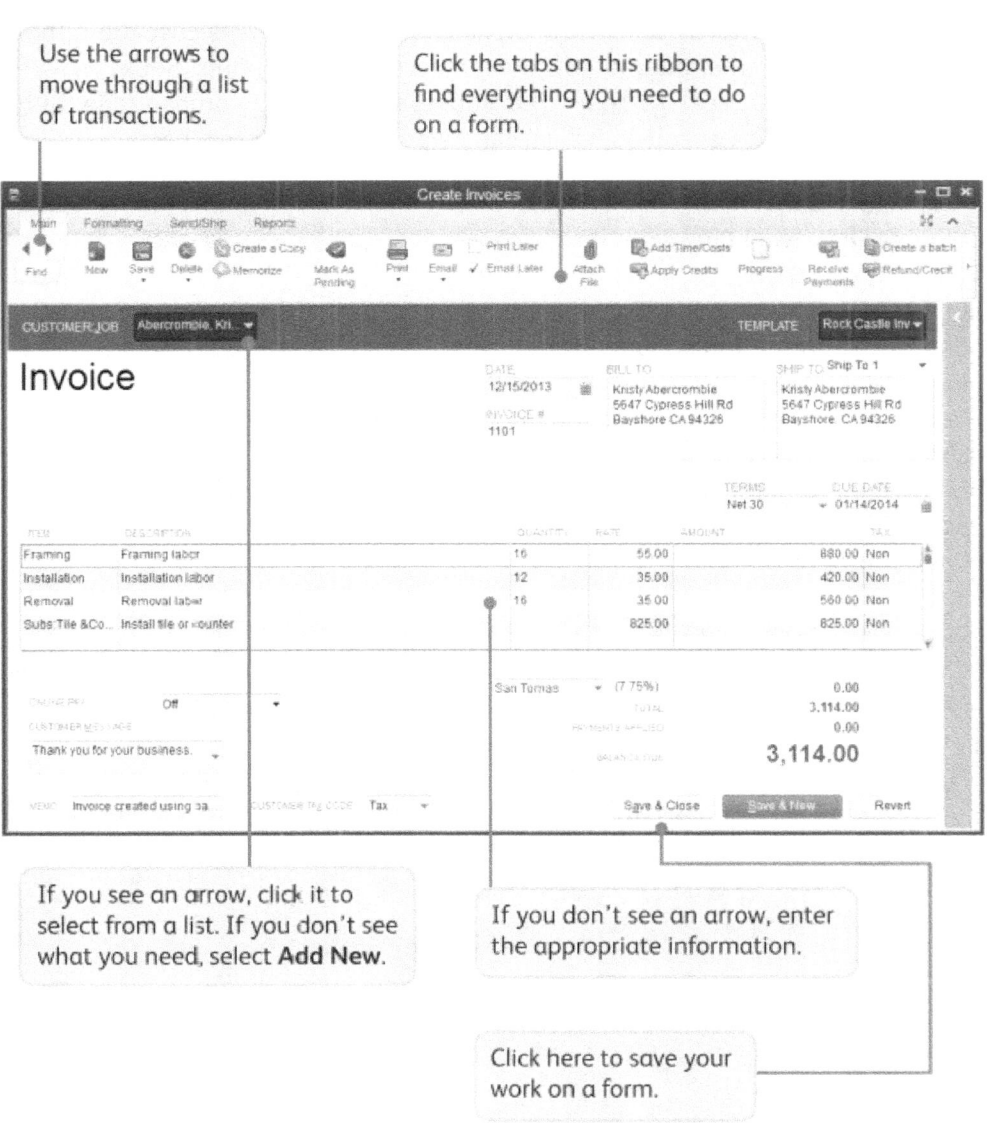

If you see an arrow, click it to select from a list. If you don't see what you need, select **Add New**.

If you don't see an arrow, enter the appropriate information.

Click here to save your work on a form.

Chart of Accounts

When you start a new company file, QuickBooks creates a preset chart of accounts based on your type of business. You can customize the chart of accounts by adding, modifying, or deleting accounts as needed.

To create a new company file with a blank chart of accounts, select the options that will minimize the number of preset accounts that QuickBooks creates. QuickBooks will still create a chart of accounts for the new company file, but it will contain only a few accounts, which can be deleted or marked inactive.

1. Open QuickBooks
2. Choose **File** > **New Company**.
3. Click **Express Start**.
4. Create the new company file:
5. Enter the information about your business.
6. Enter your Company Name.
7. Enter your Industry. Click **Help Me Choose**, scroll to the bottom of the list, and choose **Other/None.**
8. Enter your Company Type.
9. Enter your Tax ID Number.
10. Click **Continue.**
11. Enter your business contact information.
12. Click **Create Company File.**
13. Click **Start Working**.
14. Choose **Lists** > **Chart of Accounts**.
15. Your Chart of Accounts will contain only five accounts.
    - If you will not use payroll, you can make the payroll accounts inactive.
    - You can delete the other accounts, but it's strongly recommended that you do not.

Cost Code Systems

QB comes with a very basic cost code list (Lists menu -> Item List). It's best to create your own cost code/item list so that it accurately reflects what your company does.

The Cost Codes pre-installed in the Template File can be found here:
http://www.powertoolssoftware.com/QBManualMasterCode.html

Backup Company Data

Your data is valuable! No recovery technique can repair all possible file damage or protect against theft or natural disasters.

To guard against and minimize data loss, you should make regular backup copies of your QuickBooks Company (or companies). In the event of data loss, you can restore your data from the backup.

When it comes to backing up your company file, you have several options. You can backup to:

- Your Hard Drive
- Tape
- 3.5 Floppy Disks
- CD-R or CD-RW
- Zip Disk
- A secure server on the internet, if you subscribe to the QuickBooks backup service.

Note: QuickBooks Backup Service is an online backup through the Internet. t's fast and convenient, and stores a copy of your company file on secure, third-party server away from the physical location of your company.

Condensing Company File

If your company file has grown very large, you can reduce its size by condensing the older transactions that you no longer need much detail about.

For example, you might want to condense the transactions your company completed two years ago or more, especially if your company file has grown quite large (more than 75 MB). Condensing large company files can sometimes improve the performance of QuickBooks.

When you condense data, you can specify an ending date for the period of time you want to condense. Transactions dated after your selected ending date is not affected. For example, if your ending date is 12/31/12, all transactions dated 01/01/13 and later remain intact in your company file.

When you condense your company file based on transactions as of a specific date, QuickBooks deletes only closed transactions. Open transactions are retained. Therefore, to condense the most possible transactions, try to complete any unpaid bills or un-cleared transactions you have before starting. It is best to choose an end date that is six months or more in the past.

Reconciling Bank and Credit Card Accounts

Follow these steps to reconcile accounts:
1. Print your bank or credit card statement and grab a highlighter.
2. Open up QuickBooks and click on "Banking" from the top menu.

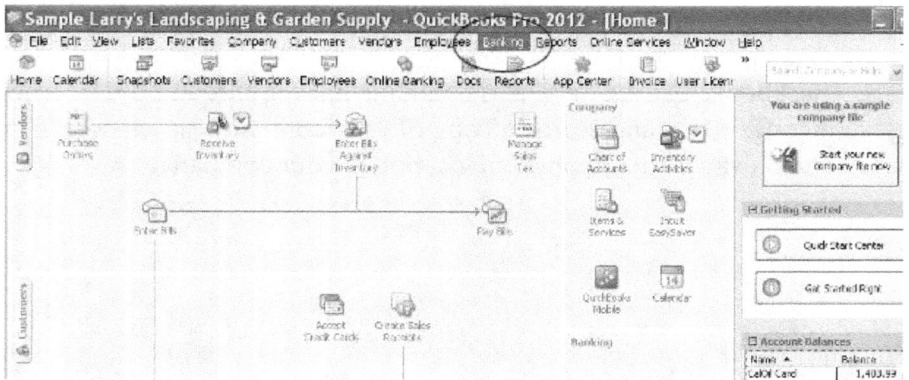

16

3. Click on "Reconcile".

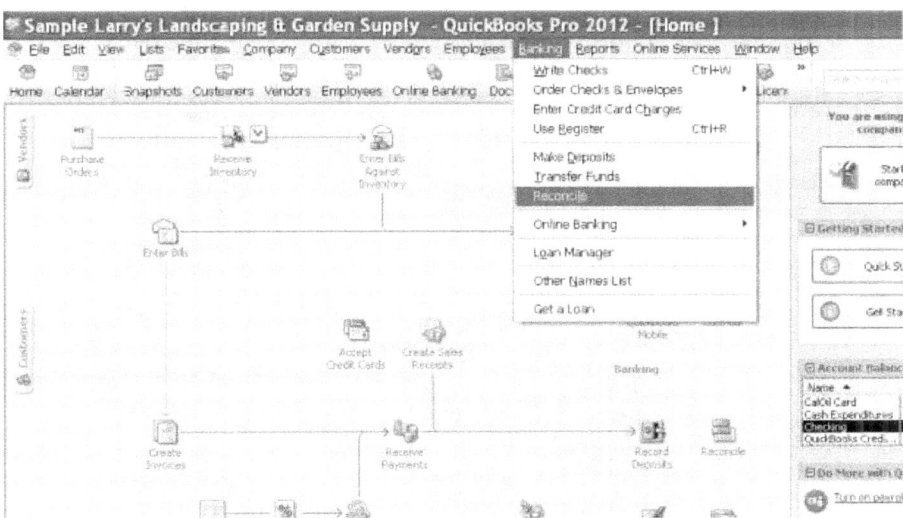

4. Select the appropriate account
5. Enter the statement end date.
6. Enter the statement ending balance.
7. Click "Continue".

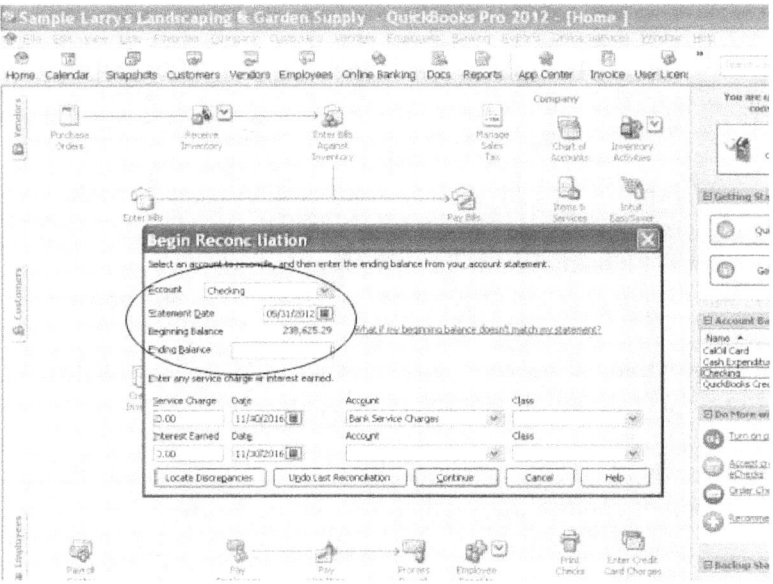

Getting Around QuickBooks Basics

8. You will see a list of checks and payments on the left and a list of deposits and credits on the right. Compare these transactions to those on your bank statement.

9. If the transactions match, put a check mark next to the transaction in QuickBooks, and highlight the transaction on your printed statement.

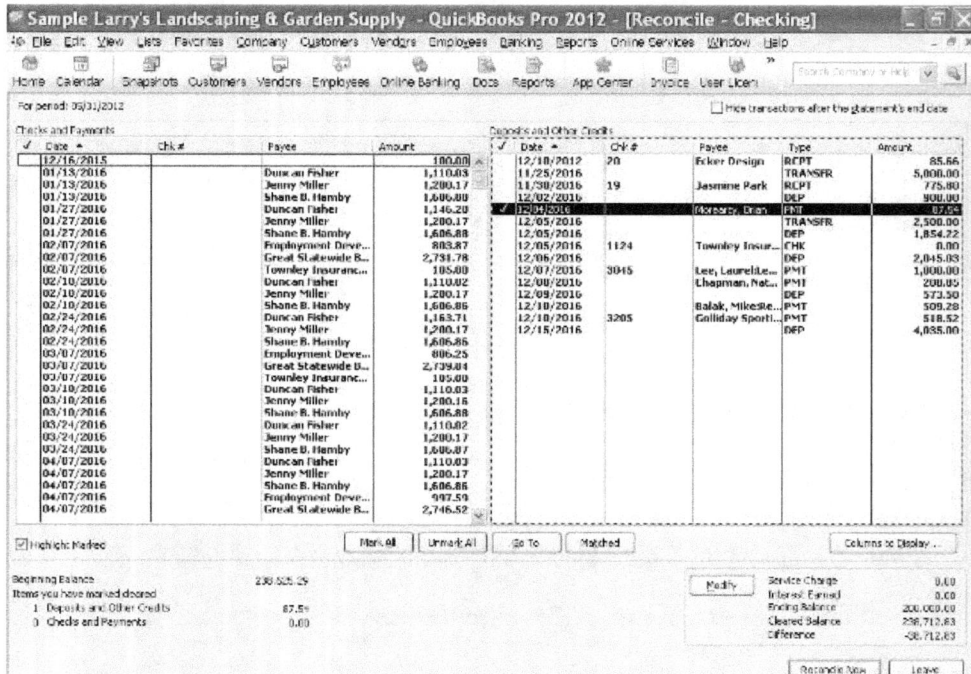

10. If you need to add, remove, or edit a transaction, click on "Leave" on the bottom right of your screen. To get back to the reconciliation screen, repeat the steps above. (Some of the information will be saved.)

11. After all items have been checked off, look at "Difference" on the bottom right.

  a. If it's zero, everything is matching up perfectly. Click on "Reconcile Now" Follow the prompts to print or save the report (if desired), or click on "Cancel". You are done.

  b. If it's not zero, there must be a missing or incorrect transaction. Review your bank statement and the transactions to find the error.

Getting Around QuickBooks Basics

Working with Multiple Users

In all versions of QuickBooks, you can set up your company file so that different users have different access to features. You can set up as many users as you want.

In QuickBooks Pro or better, several people can work with your company file at the same time over a computer network. In QuickBooks Pro and QuickBooks Premier Editions, five users can access your company file simultaneously.

Gathering Income Tax Information

As you set up your company in QuickBooks, you select which tax form your business uses:

- The T1 General form, for individuals, unincorporated businesses, and partnerships; or
- The T2 form, for incorporated businesses.

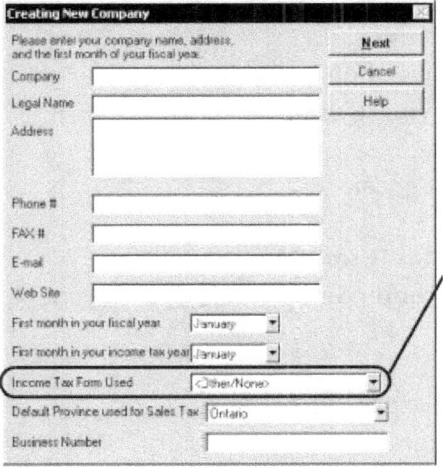

You can select a tax form either in the EasyStep Interview (as you set up your company) or in the Company Information window (from the Company menu, choose Company Information).

It's important to select the correct tax form for your business as you set it up in QuickBooks — changing it later can be very time consuming.

If you change your tax form (for example, from T1 to T2), all the mapping between your accounts and tax lines is lost.

Solving Printing Problems

If you're having trouble printing, try checking these areas before you call technical support. You can also visit http://www.quickbooks.ca/ for information about specific printers.

When Should I Reinstall My Printer Driver?

If your printer has any of these problems, you may have to reinstall your printer driver in Microsoft® Windows or contact the printer's manufacturer for assistance:

- Your printer isn't printing at all, from any program.
- Your printer prints "garbage" from any program.
- Your printer won't feed paper correctly.

Nothing Happens When You Try To Print

There are several things you can try:

- Make sure the printer is turned on and is online.
- Try printing from another application to verify that Windows can still communicate with the printer.
- Check for stalled printing jobs on your printer:
   a. From the Start menu, select Settings, then Printers.
   b. In the list, double-click the printer you're using.
   c. Select the stalled print job in the list.
   d. From the Document menu, select Cancel.

Dates and the Bottoms of Letters Are Clipped On Forms

The font you're using may be too large. In the Printer Setup window, click Font. Try a font size of 10 points or less.

Changing Fonts

1. From the File menu, choose Printer Setup.
2. Choose the form you want from the Form Name drop-down list.

Note: You can't change the fonts on some forms here. You can't change the fonts on some forms here. You can change the fonts on these forms by clicking the Customize button on the forms.

3. Click the Fonts tab and then the Font button.

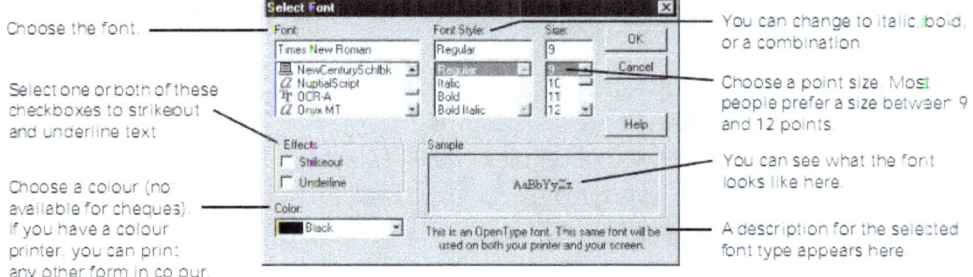

Choose the font.

Select one or both of these checkboxes to strikeout and underline text.

Choose a colour (no available for cheques). If you have a colour printer, you can print any other form in colour.

You can change to italic, bold, or a combination.

Choose a point size. Most people prefer a size between 9 and 12 points.

You can see what the font looks like here.

A description for the selected font type appears here.

4. Choose the font you want.

5. Click OK in the Select Font window and the Printer Setup window to save the changes.

Tracking Sales Tax

If you need to track sales tax on purchases (expenses, accounts payable), this must be tracked manually. QuickBooks is not setup to track sales tax automatically on non-sales transactions (such as bills, checks, and purchase orders).

How to fix it

Tracking sales tax on purchases as an expense (not to be paid later)

1. Create an expense account

2. When creating a transaction (like a bill) in which you will be tracking sales tax, enter the bill as usual, but then go to the Expenses tab and select the expense account you just created

3. On this line, enter the amount of sales tax in the Amount column (this will need to be calculated manually)

4. Ensure that any detail in this transaction adds up to the correct total after clicking Recalculate

Tracking sales tax on purchases as a liability (to be paid later)

1. Create an Other Current Liability account

2. When creating a transaction (like a bill) in which you will be tracking sales tax, enter the bill as usual, but then go to the Expenses tab and select the liability account you just created

3. On this line, enter the amount of sales tax in the Amount column (this will need to be calculated manually)

---

4. Ensure that any detail in this transaction adds up to the correct total after clicking Recalculate
5. When it is time to pay this sales tax, you can see the liability that has been accrued by looking at the Chart of Accounts
6. This amount can be paid with a regular check, selecting the liability account used for tracking this tax under the Expenses tab

Doing Business Internationally

If you deal internationally, turn on the preference for multicurrency.

In QuickBooks, from the Edit Menu, choose Preferences. Now you can customize QuickBooks for your needs.

Payroll and Employees

To pay employees, follow these steps:

1. Choose Employees > Pay Employees > Scheduled Payroll
QuickBooks displays the Employees Center window.

2. Start the Scheduled Payroll You Want To Run
To start the scheduled payroll run you want to run, click the scheduled payroll shown in the list box that appears at the top of the Employee Center window. Then choose the Start Scheduled Payroll button.

3. Use The Check Date Box To Supply The Date That You Want To Appear On Payroll Checks.
Identify the date on which the payroll period ends in the Pay Period Ends box.

4. Use the Bank Account Drop-Down List to Identify the Bank Account on Which You Want To Write Checks

5. Verify the Employees Whom You Want To Pay
QuickBooks lists the active employees included in the scheduled payroll. You want to make sure that the list of selected employees is right. You can click listed employees to select and unselect them.

6. Click Continue
QuickBooks calculates the payroll checks and payroll deduction amounts for each of the employees selected. To accept the previewed paychecks described or shown in the dialog box, click its Create Paychecks button.

7. Click the Print Paychecks or Print Pay Stubs Button
After you click the Create Paychecks button, QuickBooks displays a dialog box that lets you either print paychecks or pay stubs for direct deposit. Click the appropriate button and follow the on-screen instructions.

You should confirm the bank account from which you want to write the checks. If you're printing checks, you should also use the First Check Number box to supply the preprinted form number shown on the first payroll check that you'll print

8. Distribute the Paychecks or Pay Stubs
Obviously, after you print the checks, you sign and then distribute them.

Time Tracking
QuickBooks Pro and better provide time-tracking capability to suit your needs:

> ➤ The Stopwatch: When you're working in QuickBooks and want to take a stopwatch approach (that is, turn on a timer, work, and then stop the timer), use the Stopwatch on the Time/Enter Single Activity window.
> ➤ The QuickBooks Timer: The Timer is a separate program that runs on Windows on any computer. Because it's separate, you can distribute copies of the Timer to people who don't have access to QuickBooks, such as employees and subcontractors. Then you can merge their time data into the QuickBooks company file.

You can also enter time data manually into QuickBooks in the Weekly Timesheet window or Time/Enter Single Activity window. Tracking time can help you make better decisions about work capacity, future hiring needs, and employee productivity.

Furthermore, if you track the time you, your employees, or your subcontractors spend on each job, you'll be able to do the following:

- Invoice customers based on the number of hours of work done for them.
- Automatically fill in hours on pay checks.
- When paying subcontractors, automatically fill in hours on checks and bills.
- Track payroll costs by job, class, or type of work.
- Report hours worked by person, job, or type of work.
- Track billable versus non-billable time.

Importing and Exporting Data

Converting Data from Quicken

When QuickBooks converts a Quicken data file, it doesn't change it in any way. Also, QuickBooks does not create any sort of link between your Quicken data and your new QuickBooks Company. Instead, QuickBooks creates a completely new set of files for you to use.

Follow these steps

1. If your Quicken file is protected with a password, start Quicken, and then remove the password. If you're not sure how, check the documentation that came with your Quicken software for instructions.
2. Exit from Quicken if it is running.
3. Install QuickBooks. Instructions on installing QuickBooks are included in the "Installing & Learning to Use QuickBooks Guide".
4. Open QuickBooks by double-clicking the QuickBooks icon on your desktop.
5. From the File menu, select Import, then convert from Quicken. The Important Documentation window appears.
6. Click View Help for information about converting from Quicken.
7. Close the help window, and then click OK.
8. Choose the Quicken file you want to convert, and then click Open.
9. Follow the instructions on your screen to convert your file.

Note: After you convert your data from Quicken, you may need to fine-tune you data before you start using QuickBooks.

Converting Data from MYOB

Before converting, verify and optimize your MYOB company file to ensure that there are no data integrity issues with your data. If there are data integrity issues, the need to be resolved before you can convert to QuickBooks.

To convert MYOB data to QuickBooks follow the steps below:
1. Open QuickBooks. The Welcome to QuickBooks window appears.
2. Click the Convert from button, then select MYOB. The MYOB to QuickBooks Assistant appears.
3. Follow the onscreen instructions to convert the data in your MYOB file.

The assistant does not change anything in your original MYOB company file; it only reads the data from your MYOB file.

The conversion process may take some time depending on the size of your company file. When the assistant is done converting your data, the "Congratulations" window is displayed. At this time, you can view the log fi e to see the results of the conversion.

Click the Finish button to close the assistant and start using QuickBooks.

Importing From/ Exporting To Other Formats

QuickBooks can import information directly from some bookkeeping packages. To start the import wizard, from the File Menu, select Import, then the software you are importing from. For help, click the Help button in the wizard.

If you use QuickBooks Pro or better, with a few clicks, you can import your contacts from Microsoft Outlook or Symantec ACT!

For all other software, QuickBooks imports data in a format called IIF (Intu t Interchange Format), a special type of ASCII text file with headings to tell QuickBooks the type of information it contains. (This format is different from .QIF, used by Quicken.) If you want to import data from other software programs, you need to create an IIF file from it or reformat data you already use to conform to IIF standards.

Note: Creating an IIF file from scratch or changing data from another accounting program into an IIF file is not recommended unless you have programming experience. However, you do not need to learn about the IIF format to export lists and import them back into QuickBooks (see below).

Exporting To Other Software

When you export a list from QuickBooks, it is automatically formatted as an IIF file. You can then import the IIF file into spreadsheets, word processors, database programs, or other QuickBooks companies. You can't export transactions from QuickBooks, but you can create a report based on transactions and print it to a file that another program can import.

Everyday Tasks

Get Paid:

Create Sales Receipts

Use a sales receipt if customers pay you at the time of sale.

To start, go here: **Customers > Sales Receipts**.

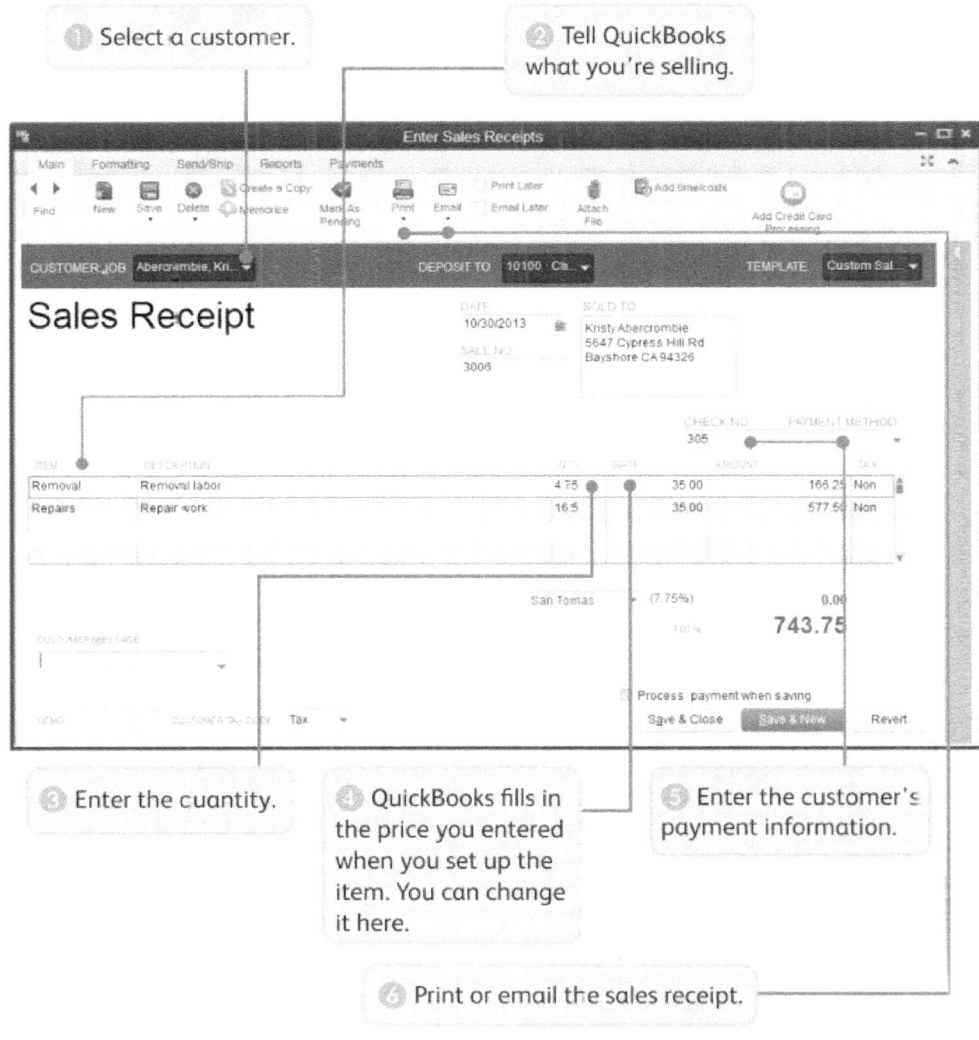

① Select a customer.

② Tell QuickBooks what you're selling.

③ Enter the quantity.

④ QuickBooks fills in the price you entered when you set up the item. You can change it here.

⑤ Enter the customer's payment information.

⑥ Print or email the sales receipt.

Create Invoices

Use an invoice when customers pay you after a sale.

To start, go here: **Customers > Create Invoices**.

Receive Payments

When a customer pays you, use the Receive Payments form to apply it to the right invoice.

To start, go here: **Customers > Receive Payments**.

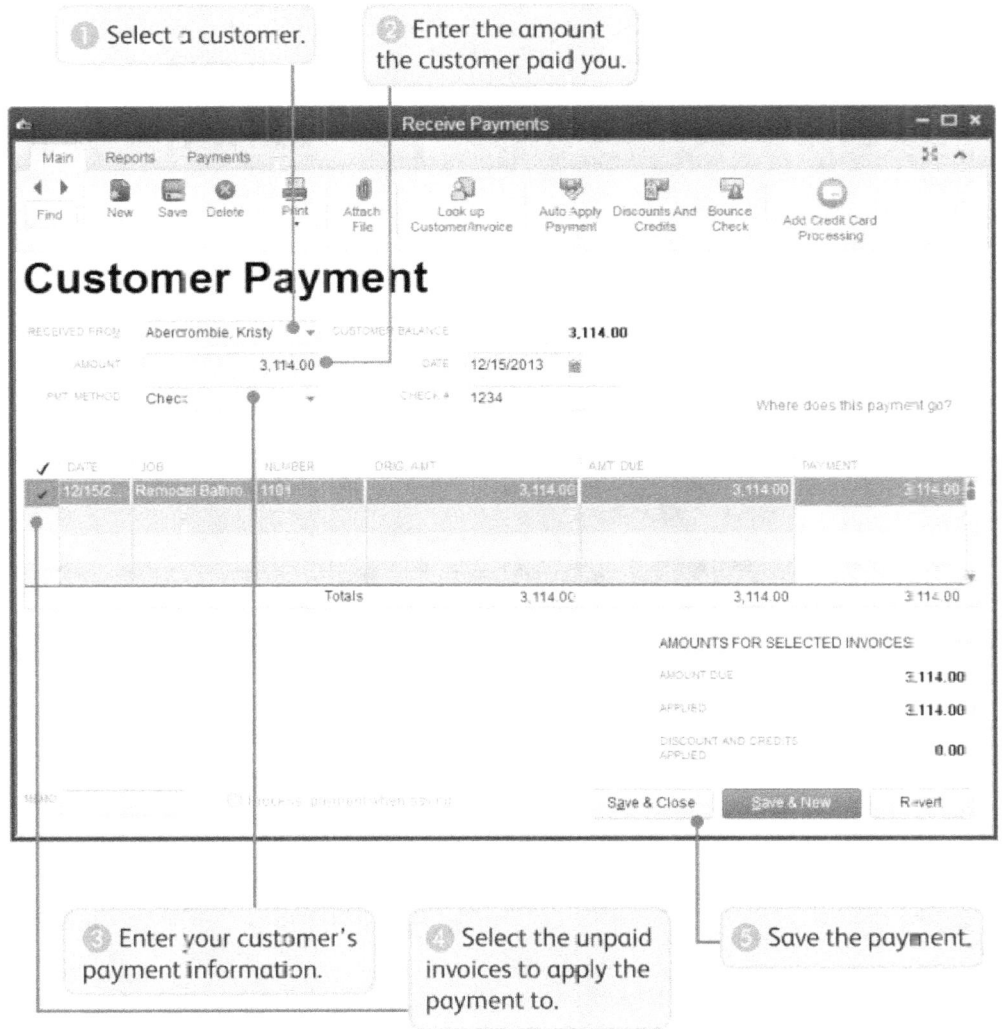

① Select a customer.

② Enter the amount the customer paid you.

③ Enter your customer's payment information.

④ Select the unpaid invoices to apply the payment to.

⑤ Save the payment.

Make Deposits

Once you've received a customer payment, you need to tell QuickBooks what bank account to deposit the money into. You do this on the Make Deposits form.

To start, go here: **Banking > Make Deposits**.

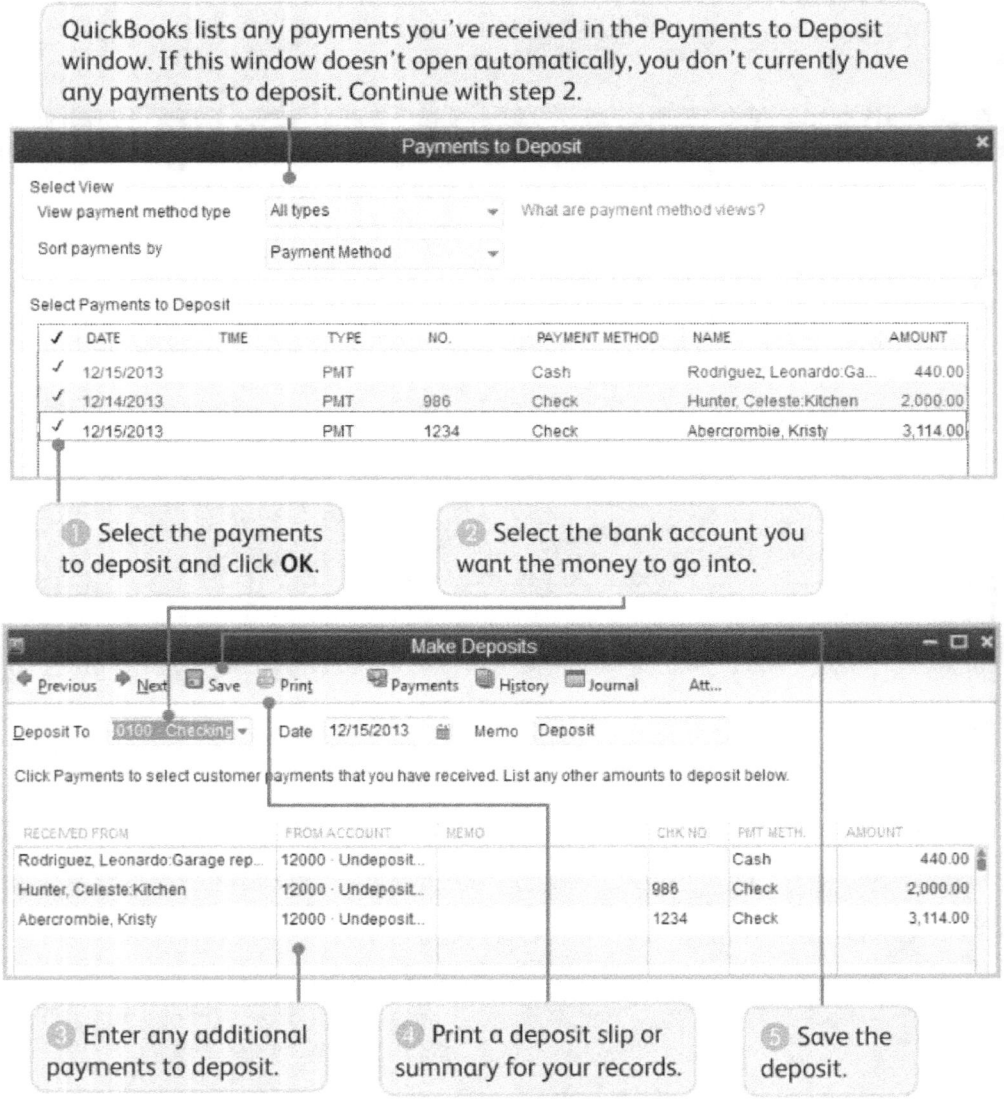

QuickBooks lists any payments you've received in the Payments to Deposit window. If this window doesn't open automatically, you don't currently have any payments to deposit. Continue with step 2.

Payments to Deposit

Select View

View payment method type   All types   What are payment method views?

Sort payments by   Payment Method

Select Payments to Deposit

✓	DATE	TIME	TYPE	NO.	PAYMENT METHOD	NAME	AMOUNT
✓	12/15/2013		PMT		Cash	Rodriguez, Leonardo:Ga...	440.00
✓	12/14/2013		PMT	986	Check	Hunter, Celeste:Kitchen	2,000.00
✓	12/15/2013		PMT	1234	Check	Abercrombie, Kristy	3,114.00

① Select the payments to deposit and click **OK**.

② Select the bank account you want the money to go into.

Make Deposits

Previous Next Save Print Payments History Journal Att...

Deposit To 10100 · Checking ▾ Date 12/15/2013 Memo Deposit

Click Payments to select customer payments that you have received. List any other amounts to deposit below.

RECEIVED FROM	FROM ACCOUNT	MEMO	CHK NO	PMT METH.	AMOUNT
Rodriguez, Leonardo:Garage rep...	12000 · Undeposit...			Cash	440.00
Hunter, Celeste:Kitchen	12000 · Undeposit...		986	Check	2,000.00
Abercrombie, Kristy	12000 · Undeposit...		1234	Check	3,114.00

③ Enter any additional payments to deposit.

④ Print a deposit slip or summary for your records.

⑤ Save the deposit.

Pay others:

In QuickBooks, you track purchases in the Write Checks, Enter Bills, or Enter Credit Card Charges windows.

- If you use your debit card or cash to buy something, use the Write Checks window to record purchase.
- To track how much you owe, use Enter Bills. When you're ready to pay the bill, use the Pay Bills window (not the Write Checks window).

Write Checks

Use the Write Checks window if you handwrite or print a check. Don't use the Write Checks to pay bills you entered or create paychecks.

To start, go here: **Banking > Write Checks**.

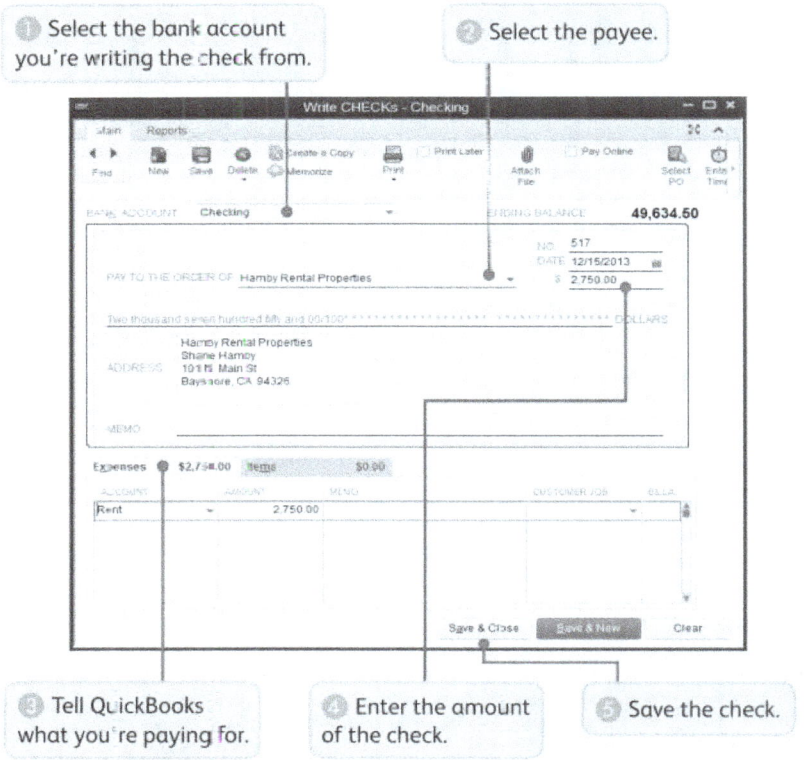

① Select the bank account you're writing the check from.

② Select the payee.

③ Tell QuickBooks what you're paying for.

④ Enter the amount of the check.

⑤ Save the check.

Enter Bills

To track how much you owe, use the Enter Bills window. Entering and paying a bill is a two-step process:

- Enter the bill using **Vendors > Enter Bills**
- Pay the bill using **Vendors > Pay Bills**

Start by entering a bill.

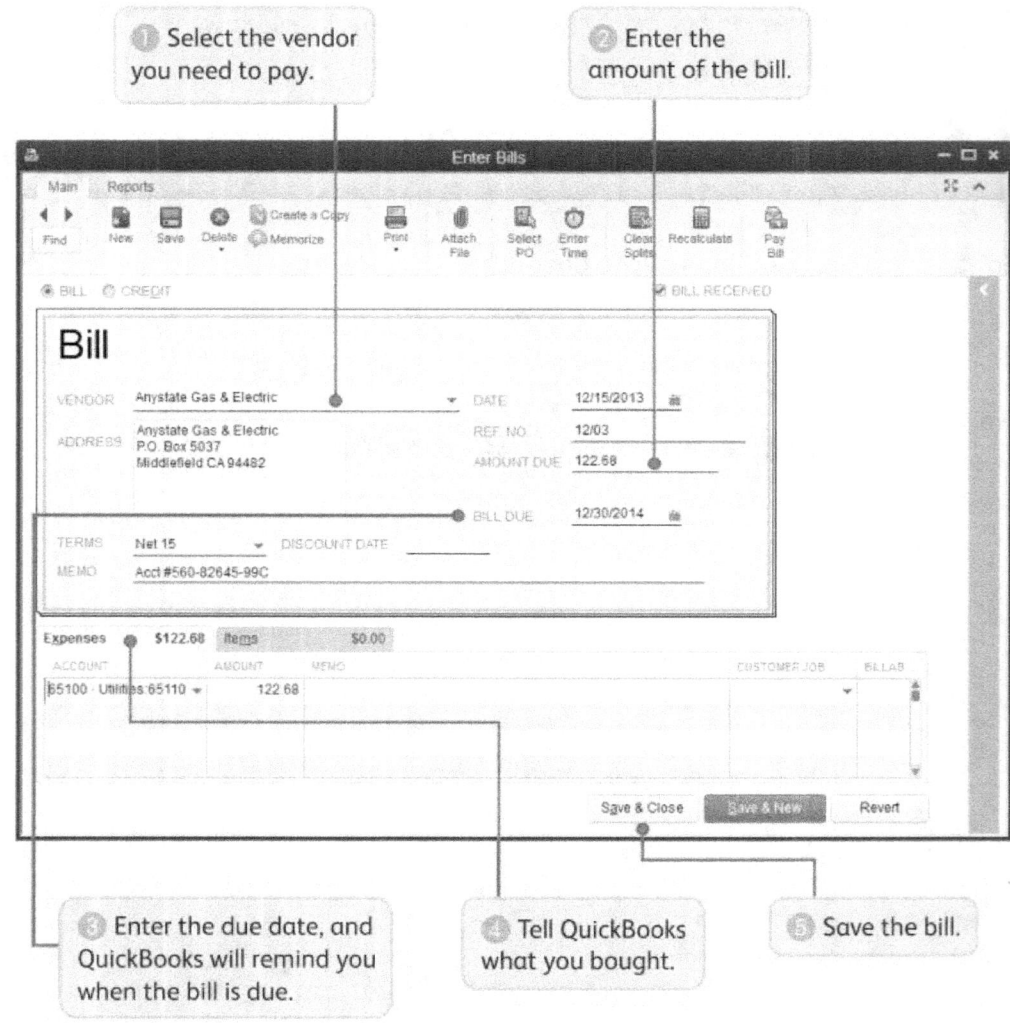

① Select the vendor you need to pay.

② Enter the amount of the bill.

③ Enter the due date, and QuickBooks will remind you when the bill is due.

④ Tell QuickBooks what you bought.

⑤ Save the bill.

Pay Bills

When you're ready to pay a bill, use the Pay Bills window.

To start, go here: **Vendors > Pay Bills**.

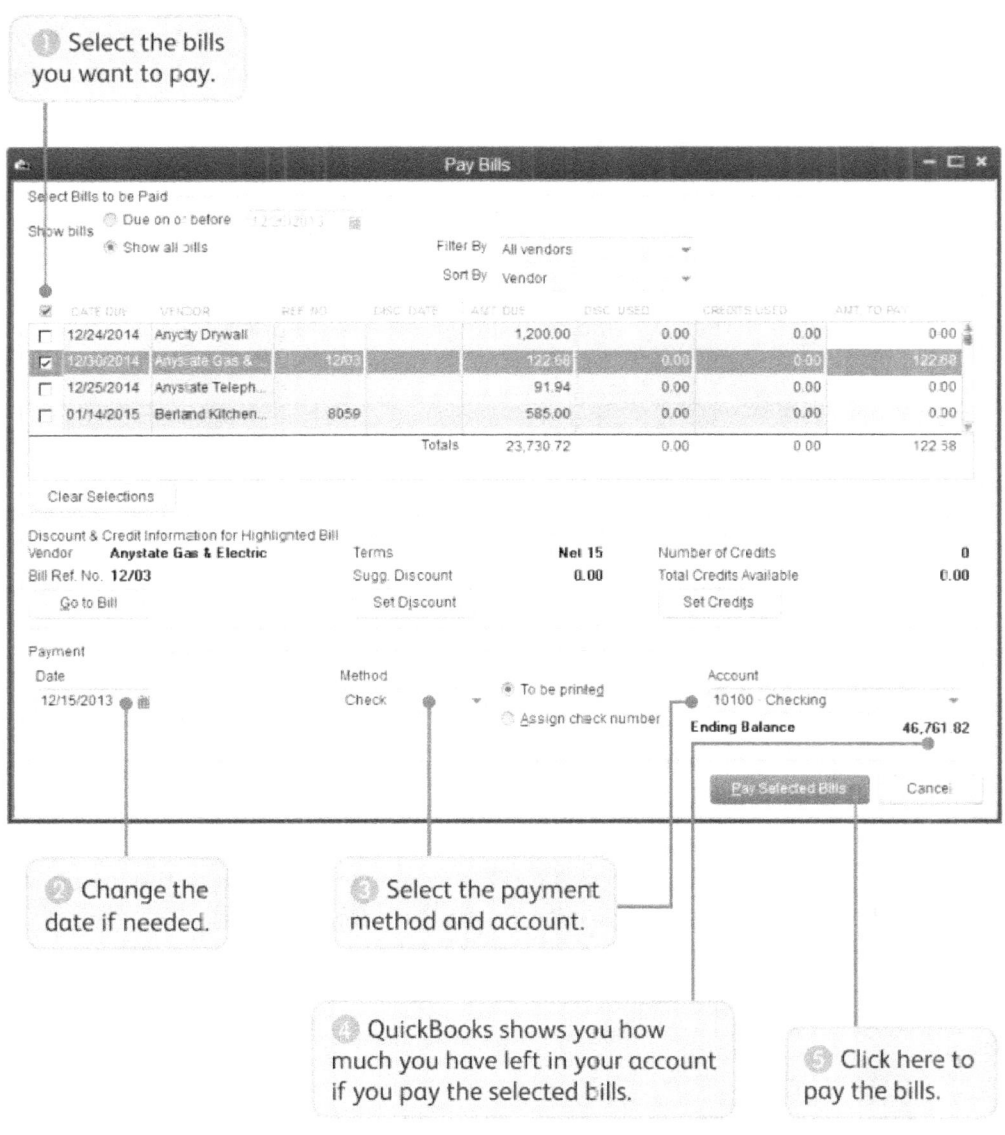

Manage Your Lists

Understanding the Items List

Every Item on the **Item List** is linked to an account on the **Chart of Accounts**. Without comprehending this relationship, the **Item List** and it's utilization in your bookkeeping system will be completely lost to you. Please review the **Item List** and the **Add New Item** or the **Edit Item** dialog box and you can observe how each Item is linked to an account from the **Chart of Accounts**, and that many of them may be linked to the same account. In other words, QuickBooks allows you to link multiple Items to the same account on the **Chart of Accounts**.

The **Items List** is designed to facilitate retail businesses that buy "items" at a wholesale price, mark them up and re-sell them at a retail price.

Using Items in QUICKBOOKS

QuickBooks makes it somewhat difficult to ignore Items altogether because of a peculiarity in the way the program is designed. When you are entering a check, bill or credit card payment, you're presented with the option of selecting the "Expenses" tab, which will post the cost to an account, or the "Items" tab, which will post the cost to an Item. However, when creating an Invoice or a Purchase Order there is no option: You cannot post an Invoice directly to an Income account, and there for you must use an Item, presumably one that is linked to an Income-account.

Sound confusing? Okay, let's take an example. Just enter the Income account number as the Item number, and you're ready to continue. For example, Item #3000 Construction Revenue is linked to Account #3000 Construction Revenue, so any invoice you write using Item #3000 will apply the amount of the invoice to Income account #3000, and thus it will be reflected on your P&L report as Construction Revenue.

Setting Up a Customer List

A Customer List keeps track of all your customers and your customer information. For example, the Customer List keeps track of billing addresses and shipping addresses for customers. Follow these steps to add a customer to the Customer List:

1. **Choose the Lists > Customer Job List command.**

   The Customer: Job button, besides letting you create new customers, provides a menu of commands for editing customer information, deleting customers, printing a customer list, and so forth.

2. **To add a new customer, click the Customer: Job button and then choose the New command.**

   QuickBooks displays the New Customer window.

3. **Use the Customer Name box to give the customer a short name.**
4. **Ignore the Opening Balance and As Of boxes.**

   You don't want to set the customer's opening balance by using the Opening Balance and As Of boxes. That's not the right way to set your new customer accounts receivable balance. If you do this, you are essentially setting up the debit part of an entry without the corresponding credit part. Later, you'll have to go in and enter crazy, wacky journal entries in order to fix your incomplete bookkeeping.

5. **Fill in the boxes of the Address Info tab.**
6. **Supply a bit of additional information about the customer.**

   - **Type drop-down list box** to categorize a customer as fitting into a particular "customer type"
   - **Terms drop-down list box** to identify the customer's default payment terms.
   - **Rep drop-down list box** to identify the customer's default sales rep.
   - **Preferred Send Method** to select the default method for transmitting the customer's invoices and credit memos.

7. **Click the Payment Info tab.**

   A set of boxes appears where you can record the customer's account number, his or her credit limit, and the preferred payment method.

Vendor List

You can add new vendors at any time. QuickBooks uses the Vendors list to hold information about the people and companies you do business with; for example, this list could include the phone company, your office supplies vendor, and your tax board.

To Add a New Vendor

1. Click the Vendors icon.
2. Click New Vendor.
3. In the Vendor Name field, enter the name of the vendor as you'd like it to appear on your Vendors list. For example, if the vendor is an individual and you list individuals by last name first, that's how you should enter the name.
4. In the Currency field, select the currency you use with this vendor. For example, if the vendor is in France, then select Euro.
5. If you have an outstanding balance for money that you owe to this vendor, enter the Opening Balance and "as of" information.
6. Enter the information requested in the Address Info tab and the Additional Info tab.
7. (Optional) On the Account Pre-fill tab, select the default expense accounts to be used for payments to this vendor.
8. (Optional) Click Next to save the vendor information and enter another vendor name.
9. Click OK to save the vendor information and close the window.

Use of Job Type List

This list holds the job types you have set up for grouping and categorizing your jobs on reports. You can add new job types to this list whenever you need them.

The Job Type list is automatically available to you when you are setting up a job (in the New/Edit Job window), or entering job information about a customer (on the Job Info tab in the New/Edit Customer window). To add a job type, click the Job Info tab in the New/Edit Customer window and fill in the Job Type field.

Manage Your Job Types

Click Job Type at the bottom of the list to add, edit, or delete job types. You can make a job type inactive, print the list, and more.

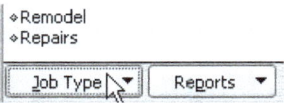

To view reports related to this list, click Reports at the bottom of the list.

Class List

You can create classes that you assign to transactions. This lets you track account balances by department, business office or location, separate properties you own, or any other meaningful breakdown of your business.

When class tracking is turned on in the Accounting Preferences window, QuickBooks adds a Class field to the windows where you enter transactions. You can fill in this field by choosing a class from your Class list.

Add Classes

1. Go to the Lists menu and choose Class List. ⛶
2. Click Class at the bottom of the list and click New.

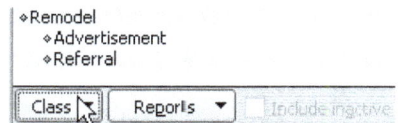

3. Enter a name for the class.
4. If you want the class to be a subclass of another class, select the Subclass of checkbox, and enter the name of the parent class.
5. Record the class.

See How Your Business Is Going:

Using the Reports Center

All of your QuickBooks information can be found, organized and presented as a report. QuickBooks has more than 100 reports, and the report Center makes it easy to find and understand the right report.

To start, go here: **Report > Reports Center.**

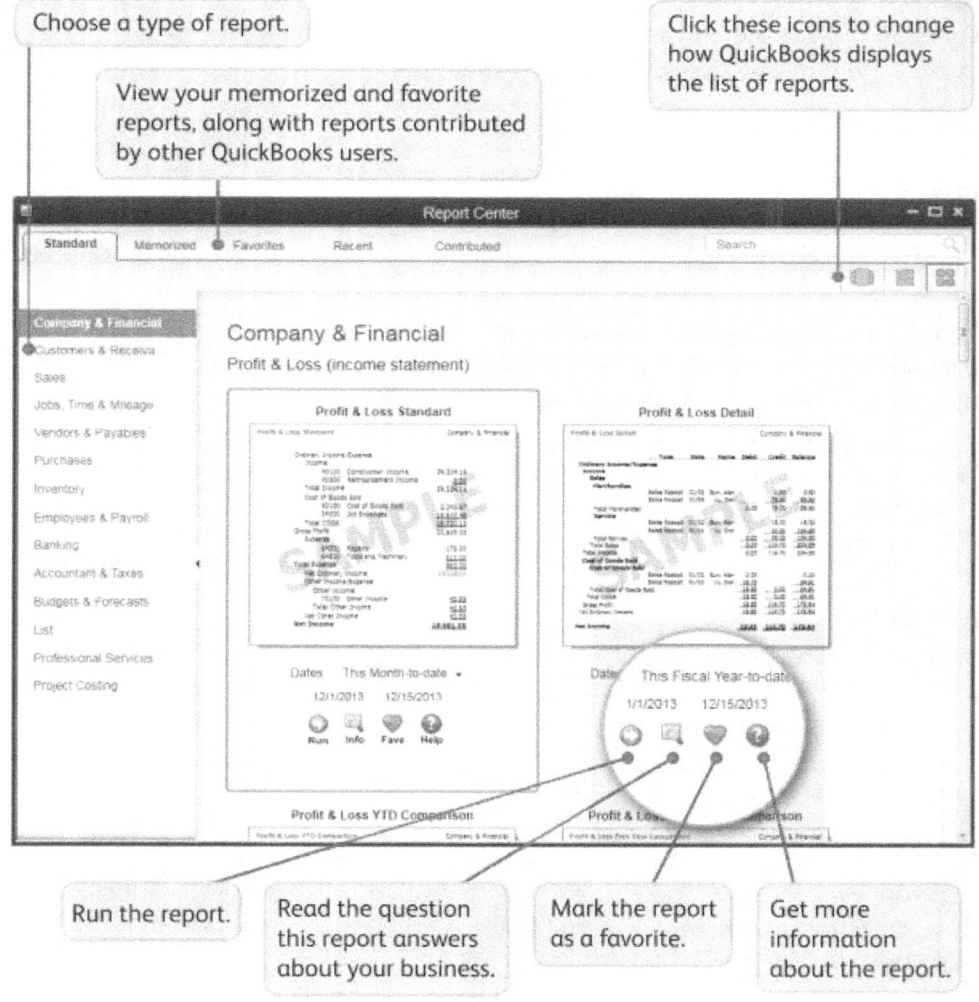

Choose a type of report.

Click these icons to change how QuickBooks displays the list of reports.

View your memorized and favorite reports, along with reports contributed by other QuickBooks users.

Run the report.

Read the question this report answers about your business.

Mark the report as a favorite.

Get more information about the report.

Company Snapshot

Use the Company Snapshot to get real-time company information and perform tasks from a single place.

To start go here: **Company > Company Snapshot.**

This is a snapshot of the money going in and out of your business over time. Use this section to compare monthly income and expenses.

Click here to learn how to customize the Company Snapshot.

See what your customers owe you.

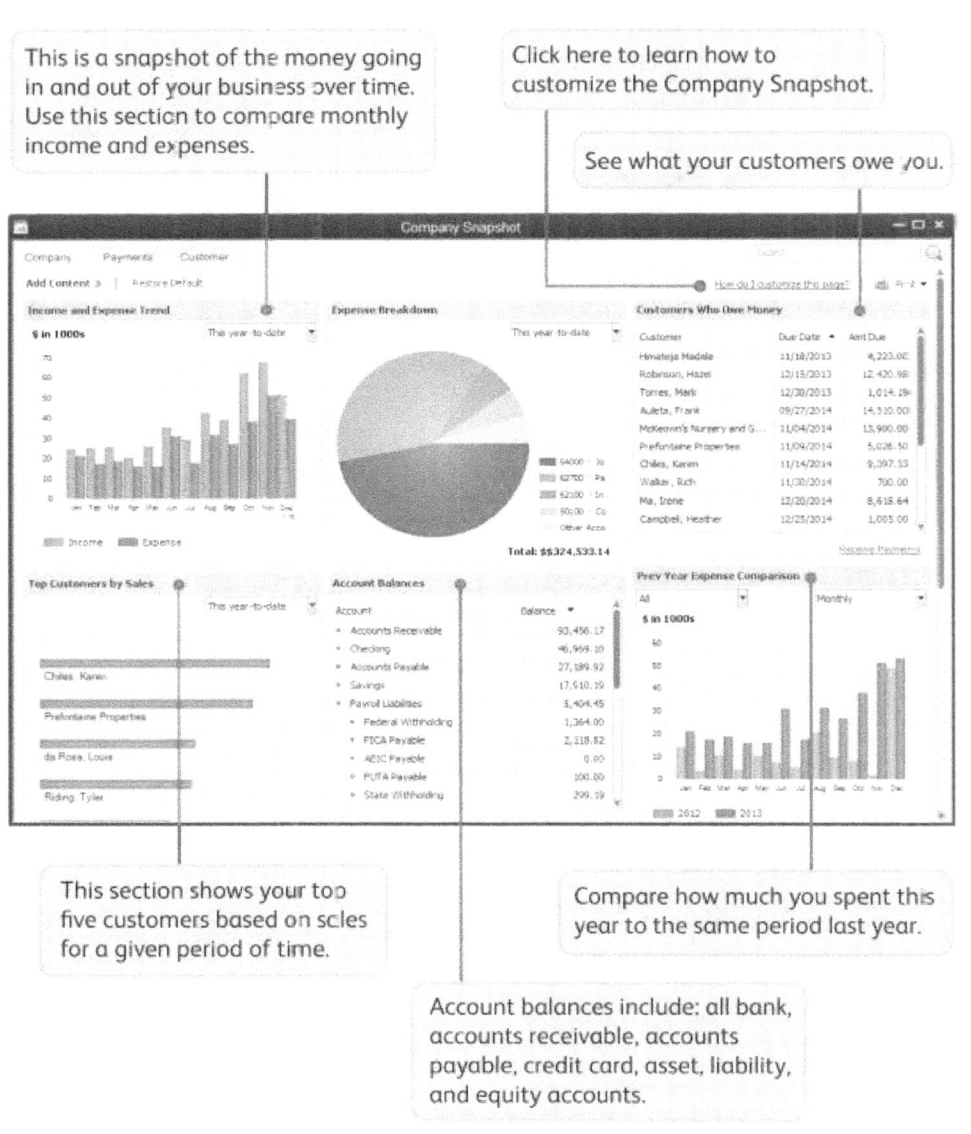

This section shows your top five customers based on sales for a given period of time.

Compare how much you spent this year to the same period last year.

Account balances include: all bank, accounts receivable, accounts payable, credit card, asset, liability, and equity accounts.

See How Your Business is Doing

Profit and Loss

This report is also known as an income statement. It summarizes your income and expenses for a particular period, so you can tell whether you're operating at a profit or a loss.

To start go here: **Reports > Company & Financial > Profit & Loss Standard.**

Click here to customize your report.

If you've customized the report and want to use it again, click here to memorize the report.

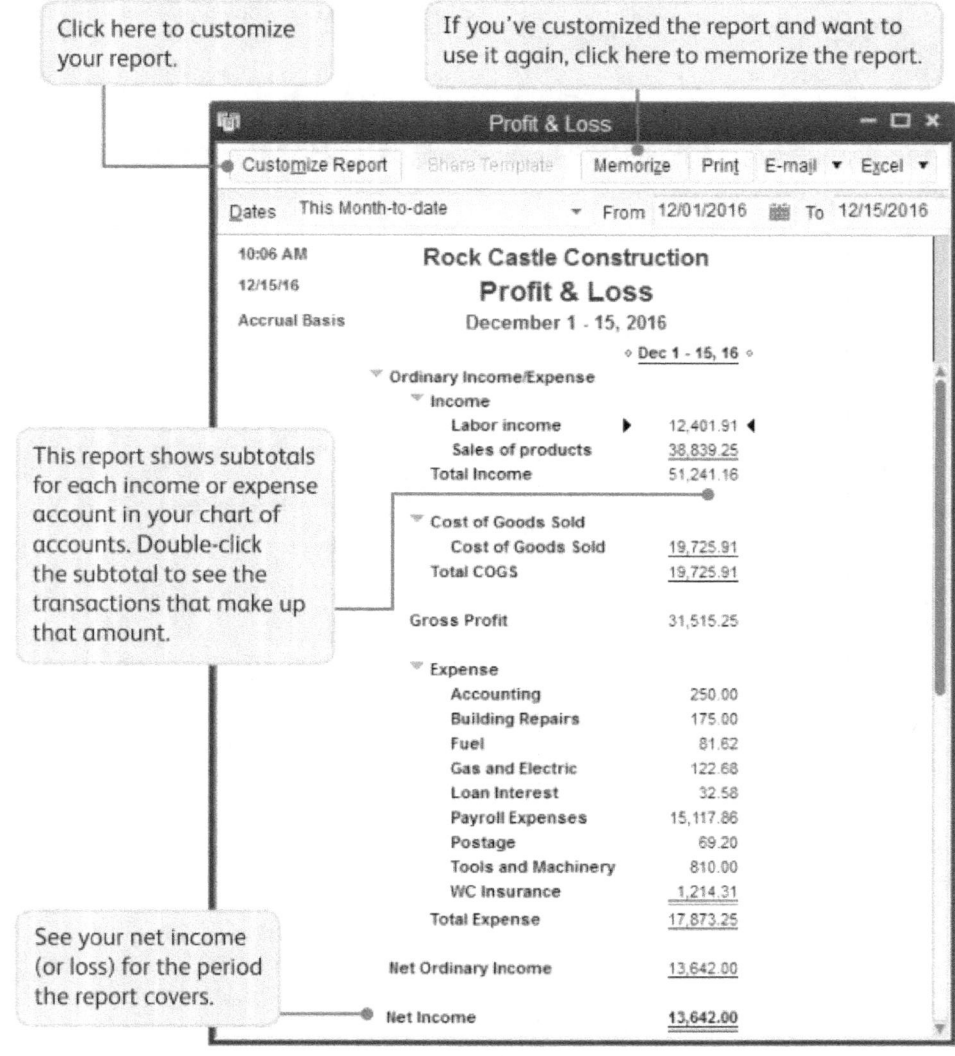

This report shows subtotals for each income or expense account in your chart of accounts. Double-click the subtotal to see the transactions that make up that amount.

See your net income (or loss) for the period the report covers.

See How Your Business is Doing

Balance Sheet

This report provides a financial snapshot of your company as of a specific date.

To start, go here: **Reports > Company & Financial > Balance Sheet Standard.**

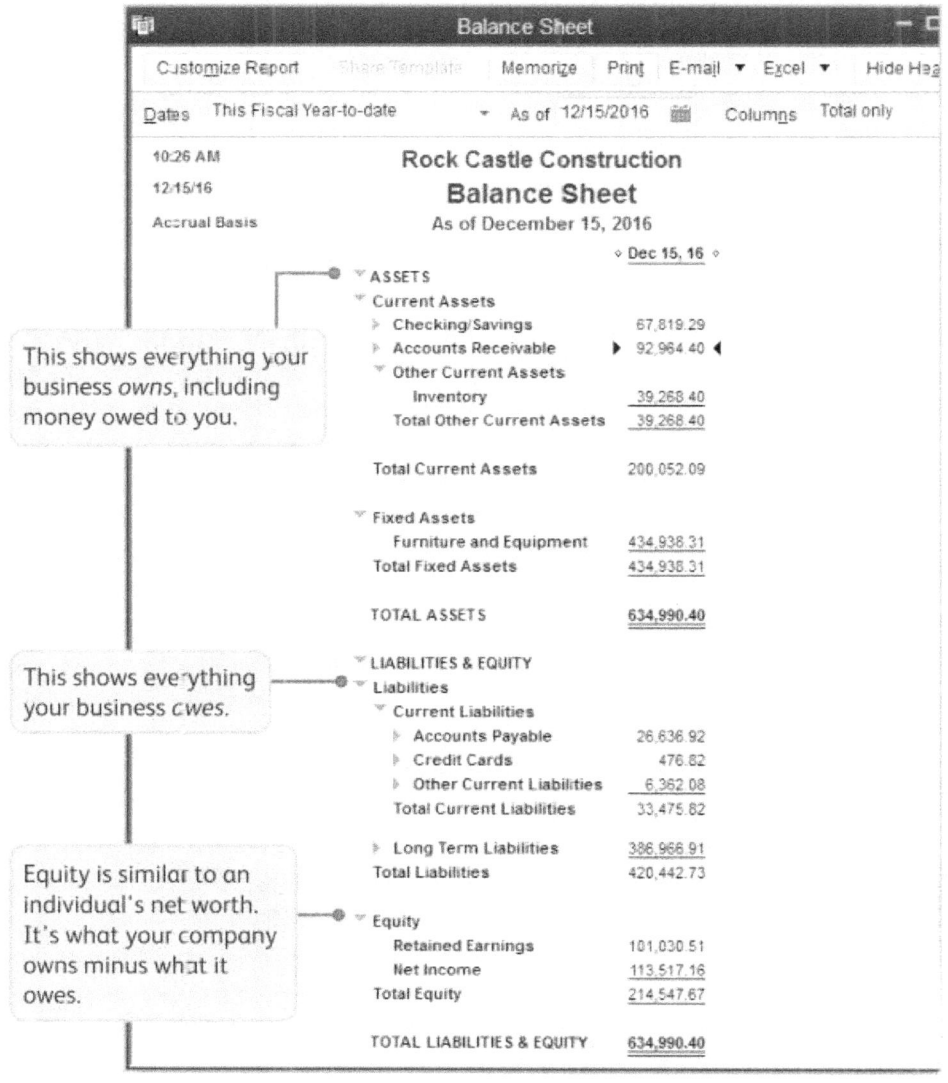

This shows everything your business *owns*, including money owed to you.

This shows everything your business *owes*.

Equity is similar to an individual's net worth. It's what your company owns minus what it owes.

See How Your Business is Doing

Boost Your Proficiency

More than 4.5 million companies use QuickBooks, making it by far the most widely used accounting system in the world. However, many CPAs frequently overlook or underutilize the product's strongest features. Are you using QuickBooks efficiently and getting the most you can out of the product? Following is a list of QuickBooks intermediate and advanced features that you should be using to boost proficiency.

Batch Invoicing

QuickBooks versions 2011 and higher enable users to create a batch of invoices in a single process. For example, a company that needs to invoice 500 customers each month for a $20 Webhosting fee can generate all 500 invoices in one step. The batch invoice feature also allows users to search for customers according to custom data fields and then invoice the resulting group. For example, this would empower the boat marina's bookkeeper (as mentioned above) to invoice in a single step each customer who subscribes to the monthly cranking service. To access the tool, go to the Customers menu, and select Create Batch Invoices (see screenshot atop the next column).

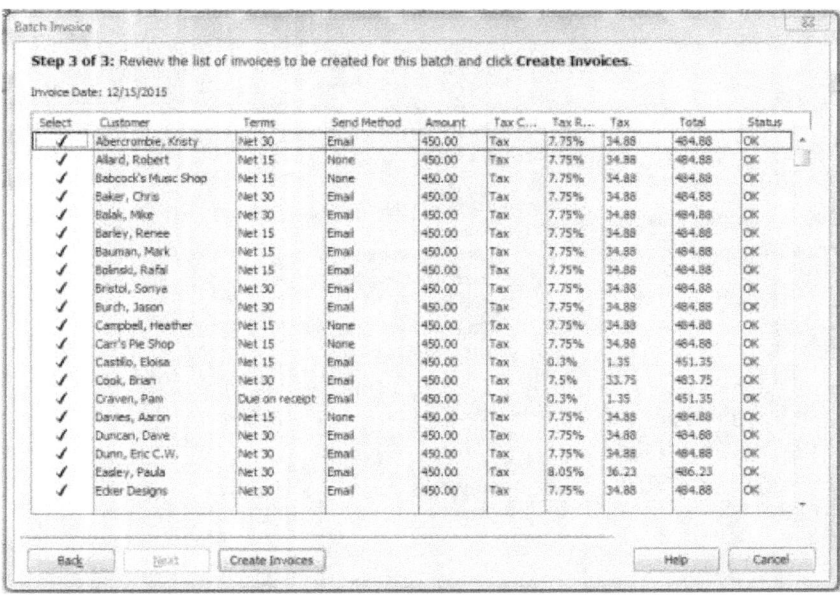

QuickBooks Loan Manager

Many small businesses record loan payment transactions improperly, failing to separate the loan payment into the proper interest and principal portions according to the loan amortization schedule. Loan Manager provides a solution that enables you to set up each loan with its associated parameters, such as term, rate, fees, compounding, balloon payments, etc. Thereafter, Loan Manager will generate the correct loan payment check each payment period, once again saving time, reducing mistakes and increasing accuracy. To access the tool, go to the Banking Menu > Loan Manager.

Memorize Transactions

For every company, a significant number of transactions recur regularly, and QuickBooks accommodates this by enabling you to memorize recurring transactions. For example, suppose a company makes the same monthly rent payment, bills clients for recurring monthly services or records the same monthly depreciation entries. In these cases, QuickBooks can memorize the transactions and automatically enter them for you at regularly scheduled intervals. This feature can help save time, reduce mistakes and increase accuracy. You also can use this feature to memorize complex journal-entry templates, such as detailed allocations, and enter the actual amounts later. To access the tool, type Ctrl + M.

Memorize Transaction Tip: Memorize Transaction will generate electronic payments or paper checks but it does not automatically send or print them. Once a check is created in QuickBooks, you can send or print the check using the File menu's Send Documents or Print Documents menu options.

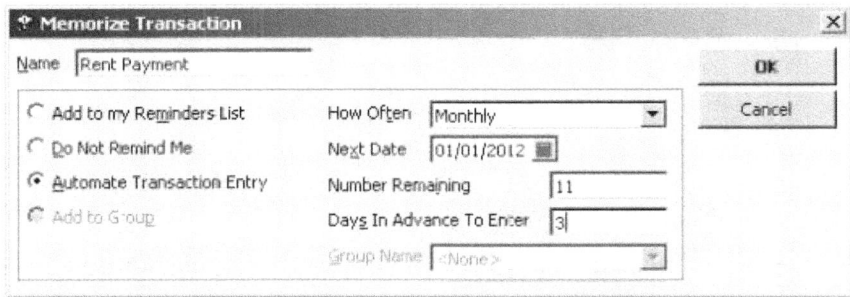

Custom Data Fields

Custom fields are one of the most powerful features in QuickBooks accounting software. QuickBooks Premier provides 20 generic custom data fields, and QuickBooks Enterprise provides more than 50 content-specific custom data fields. Using these data fields, a clever CPA can overcome many shortcomings in an accounting system. For example, a boat marina might use custom fields to track the name of the customer's boat and slip number and to create a data field indicating whether the customer subscribes to the monthly cranking service (see screenshot below).

Further, QuickBooks allows users to filter reports using those custom data fields. For example, the boat marina could filter a list of customers to display only those who subscribe to the monthly cranking service, thereby producing a list of boats that need cranking each month. To use the tool, go to the Customer Center, select a Customer, click the Edit Customer button, then under the Additional Information tab, click Define Fields.

Custom Data Tip: Information entered into custom data fields can also be included in financial reports, on invoices and in all QuickBooks documents.

Process Multiple Reports

Often, bookkeepers who do a good job of keeping the books fail to consistently produce and distribute the necessary financial reports each day, week or month for company personnel to use in managing the business. In many cases, the process of preparing and printing dozens of reports is too time-consuming.

QuickBooks provides a solution called Process Multiple Reports, which enables users to group together dozens of reports (using the Memorize function) and print them all in a single step, as shown below. To access the tool, go to the Reports menu, Process Multiple Reports.

Multiple Reports Tips: When memorizing each report, include the recipient's name in the report title to make distribution a little easier. In addition, re-sorting the reports in the Memorize Report window will ensure that the reports print in collated order.

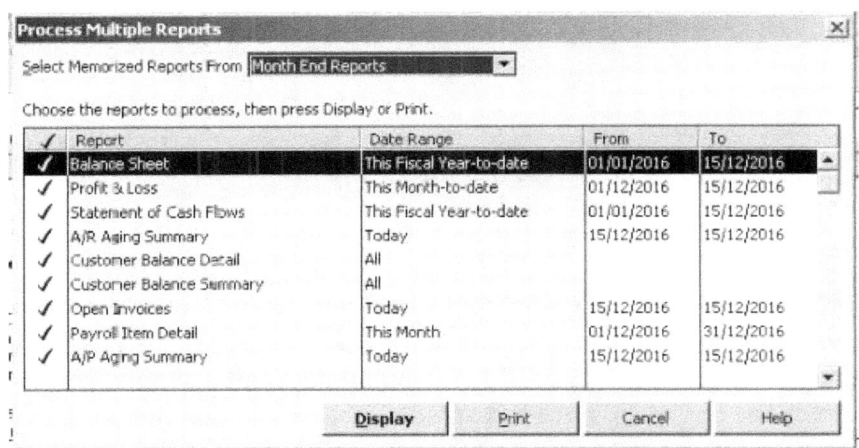

Prevent Prior-Period Changes

A common issue with QuickBooks is how easily users can (intentionally or unintentionally) enter or edit transactions in prior periods. To prevent unauthorized prior-period entries or changes, set up a unique username and password for each user and set each user's preferences to prohibit him or her from bypassing the closing date.

Thereafter, by establishing a password-protected closing date and moving it forward each month as review and adjustments are completed, you can lock down the prior-period data as the year progresses, as shown in the screenshot at the bottom of the previous page. To access the tool, go to the Company menu, Set Closing Date.

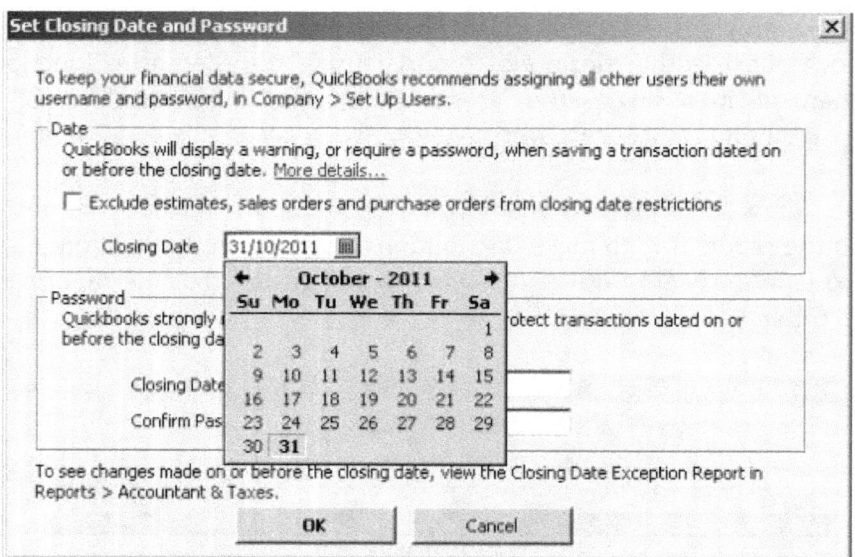

Stratifying Reports

QuickBooks provides a Columns tool that can stratify financial reports by numerous column configurations. This functionality is valuable for analyzing and scrutinizing a company's financials. For example, a single column profit-and-loss statement can be quickly transformed into an 81-column profit-and-loss statement—with a separate column for each of 80 customers and a total column at the end. Likewise, that same report could be re-stratified to display a column for each inventory item, thereby reporting the profit (or loss) for each item (or group of items). Other options include stratifying columns by month, quarter, year, departments, sales representatives and more (see screenshot below).

Surprisingly, many popular, high-end accounting systems and enterprise resource planning applications fail to provide this type of beneficial reporting. To access the Columns tool in any financial report, click on the Columns dropdown menu above the report.

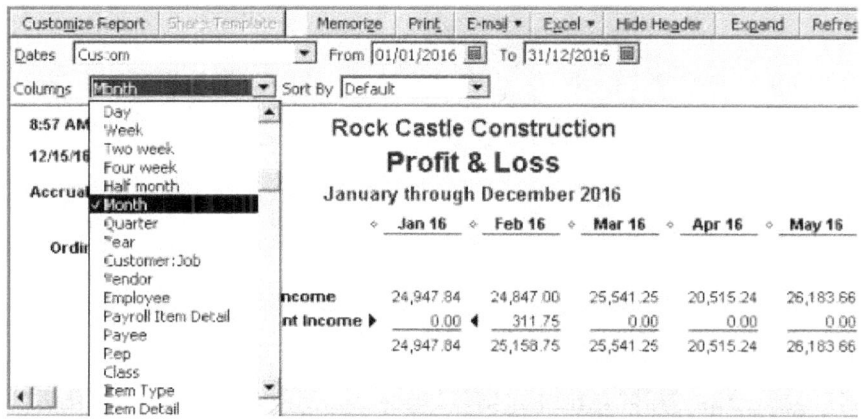

Remote Access

QuickBooks Remote Access is a Web-based service (go to http://tinyurl.com/m7ljuf) that allows CPAs to securely log in to their clients' QuickBooks systems. Remote Access grants the CPA entry only to the client's QuickBooks application and data and prevents the CPA from viewing other data, such as Word, Excel and email files, on the client's computer. The service takes only a few minutes to set up and, thereafter, the CPA can log in to the client's QuickBooks to train users, review the client's books and, if appropriate, enter corrections and adjustments.

Using Remote Access is a better solution than using the QuickBooks Accountant's Copy method, for several reasons. First, the CPA avoids the need to have the client's edition of QuickBooks running. Second, the CPA and client do not have to send the Accountant's Copy files back and forth. Third, Remote Access provides full access to the client's data in real time. Further, Remote Access makes it easier for the CPA to provide monthly and on-demand services throughout the year. In contrast, the Accountant's Copy approach often leads the CPA to be involved with the client's books only at yearend. (*Note:* Remote access is priced starting at $3.95 per month.)

Remote Access Tip: This type of remote access gives the CPA control of the client's screen, allowing the client to see the CPA's mouse actions as the client is trained remotely via the telephone.

Boost Your Proficiency

Using Account Numbers

As an option, QuickBooks allows you to display seven-digit account numbers in addition to 31-digit alphanumeric account names. The benefits are faster data entry (using a 10 key) and the ability to control the sort order of accounts displayed in financial reports. For example, you could use this feature to dictate that the accumulated depreciation account appears below property and equipment, not above. To use the tool, go to the Edit menu, Preferences, Accounting, Company Preferences tab, and check the Use account numbers box, as shown below.

However, activating this option also includes account numbers in the financial statements and reports, which is not always desirable. To suppress account numbers, edit each account and add an account description, then set the Reports-Show Accounts by preference to Description Only. After that, only the account descriptions, instead of account numbers and names, will appear on all financial statements.

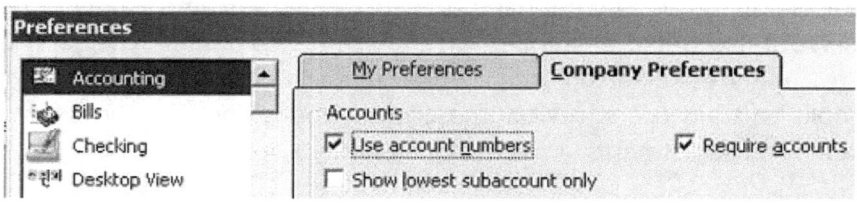

Reporting Tip: The "Description Only" preference setting can be used to display customized row descriptions on financial statements; for example, you may prefer "Trade Receivables" instead of "Accounts Receivable."

Fixed Asset Manager

Every company has assets, and the QuickBooks Fixed Asset Manager (included in the Accountant and Enterprise editions) can track those assets according to six methods (federal, state, book, adjusted current earnings, alternative minimum tax and other).

The system incorporates many tax methods, such as the accelerated cost recovery system, the modified accelerated cost recovery system, and the IRC Sec. 168(f)(1) and Sec. 179 depreciation methods, among others. Upon asset dispositions, the

---

48

system can calculate the appropriate gain or loss on sales, as well as the appropriate amounts of depreciation recapture. Although fixed-asset data can be integrated with QuickBooks, many companies tend to use the Fixed Asset Manager as a stand-alone product—which I recommend because the effort setting up integration probably takes more time than it saves during the year—and enter manual depreciation entries each month in QuickBooks. To access the Fixed Asset Manager, go to the Accountant menu, Manage Fixed Assets.

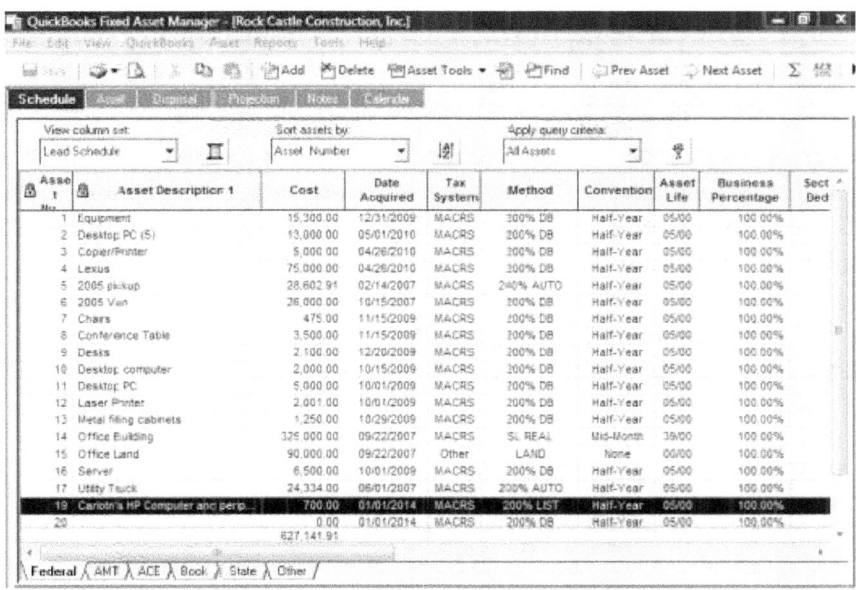

Attach Documents

The Attach Documents feature enables you to attach electronic documents throughout QuickBooks to achieve a paperless environment. As documents are processed, you can save them locally on your computer network or to a cloud-based storage facility accessible by all users, even those in remote locations.

Some of the advantages to maintaining a paperless accounting system are:

a. Electronic documents can be available to all users, even remote users;

b. You can locate electronic documents quickly via indexed searching;

c. Electronic documents are easier to include when preparing reports or email messages, reducing the costs associated with making copies and sending paper documents;

Boost Your Proficiency

d. Electronic documents can be easily backed up off-site for better data protection; and

e. Electronic documents reduce costs related to paper documents such as filing cabinets, file rooms and archiving efforts.

There used to be a charge associated with this feature, but the new QuickBooks 2012 Pro offers Attach Documents with free local storage, as Intuit is phasing out the cloud option. To use the tool, click the Attach button with the paper clip icon in any document or template. This option is grayed out until setup is completed.

Prepare Letters and Envelopes

The Prepare Letters and Envelopes tool provides an assortment of templates and mail-merge capabilities for generating custom letters targeting customers, vendors, employees and others. Examples of the included templates are "Scheduled delivery notice," "Bounced check" and "Late payment reminder." You can also use this tool to create customer-specific letters such as new products or service announcements and invitations for selected customers to attend special VIP sales events. To access the tool, go to the Company menu, Prepare Letters and Envelopes.

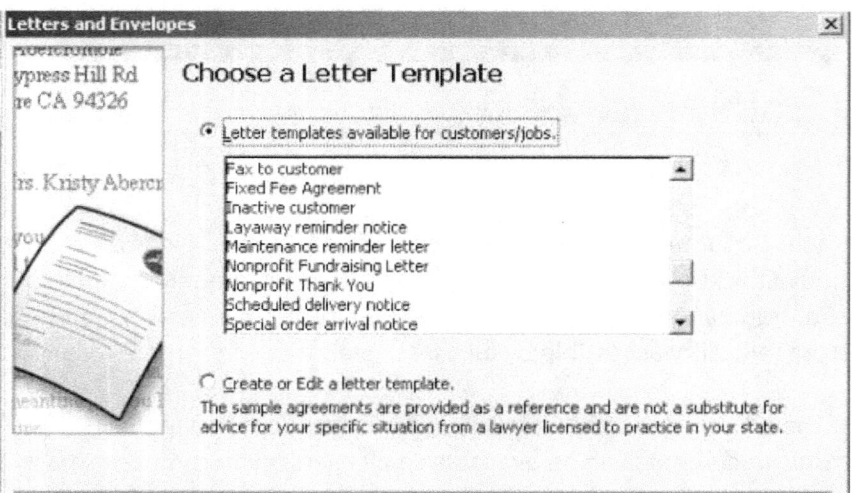

Imported Credit Card Transactions

Typing a lengthy credit card statement into your accounting system is time-consuming and difficult to accomplish without making transposition or key punching errors. By contrast, in most cases, credit card transaction data can be imported directly into QuickBooks in just a few seconds, and QuickBooks' bu lt-in logic can automatically match the expenditures with the appropriate vendor and account number for more efficient processing. This feature is included for free. To access, go to the Banking menu, Enter Credit Card Charges and click the Download Credit Card Charges option at the top of the page. Your specific setup and monthly procedures will vary depending on the credit card company you use.

QuickBooks Keyboard Shortcuts

Date Field Shortcuts

T	Today's date
+	Next day
-	Previous day
Y	First day of the year
R	Last day of the year
M	First day of the month
H	Last day of the month
W	First day of the week
K	Last day of the week

Alpha Shortcuts

Ctrl + A	Chart of Accounts
Ctrl + D	Delete Transaction
Ctrl + F	Find
Ctrl + G	Go To Other Account Register
Ctrl + H	Get Transaction History
Ctrl + I	Create Invoice
Ctrl + J	Customer Center
Ctrl + M	Memorize Transaction
Ctrl + N	New Transaction or Item
Ctrl + O	Copy Transaction in Register
Ctrl + P	Print
Ctrl + Q	Quick Report from List
Ctrl + R	Register
Ctrl + T	List of Memorized Transactions
Ctrl + W	Write Checks
Ctrl + Y	Display Transaction Journal
Ctrl + Z	Undo or Drill Down

QuickBooks Exercises

How to Add a Payroll Deduction

In this section, you create payroll items. A payroll item is anything that affects the amount of a paycheck. It also includes company expenses (like matched taxes). When you first set up payroll, the QuickBooks Payroll Setup wizard helps create your company's payroll items. You learn how during this practice exercise.

Add Payroll Item

1. You decide to offer health insurance at your company. Add the payroll item. Click the Employees menu and select Manage Payroll Items >New Payroll Item.

2. Choose the EZ Setup method and click Next.

3. Select Insurance Benefits as the type and click Next

4. QuickBooks loads the Payroll Setup Interview. Select Health insurance. Click Next.

5. QuickBooks asks how your company pays health insurance. In this case, the employee pays the full cost. Select the third option.

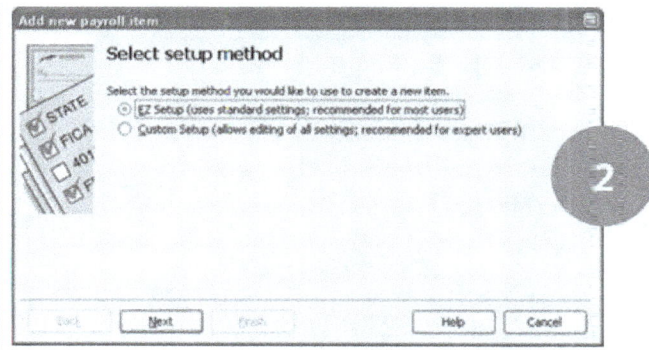

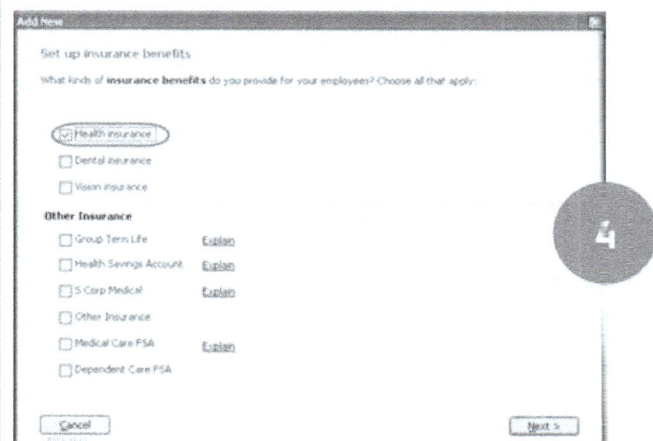

6. QuickBooks gives you two more choices. In this case, health insurance is an after-tax deduction, so click Payment is deducted after taxes and click Next. Please note: The only way you can deduct money before taxes are calculated is if Congress passed a law that allows you to do this. With certain health insurance plans, there is a law (Section 125) that allows health insurance deductions before taxes are calculated. If you're not sure, always check with an accountant.

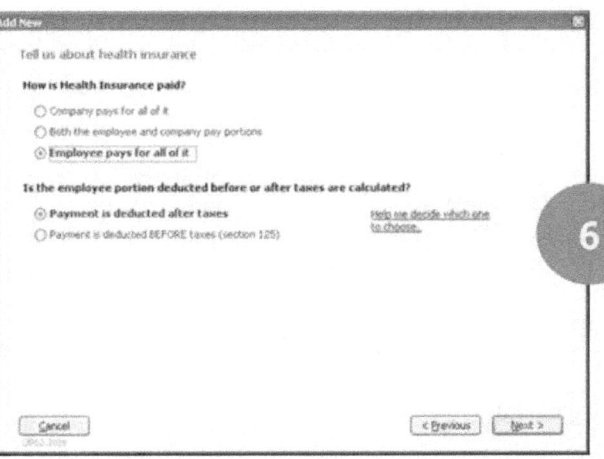

7. Next, enter information about when and who you pay for the insurance. Click the Payee drop-down list and select Sergeant Insurance.

8. Enter account number 51233. This account number appears as the Memo on the Payroll Liability check QuickBooks creates when you pay Sergeant Insurance.

54

9. Then, enter the Payment frequency for the insurance. In this case, payment is due on the 15th of the month for the prior month's insurance. Click Monthly. This step is very important. If you don't set the frequency, the Liability will not show up in the "Pay Scheduled Liabilities" section of the Payroll Center. This means you may forget to pay it!

10. Then, click the drop-down list, select 15 and click Next.

11. Click Finish.

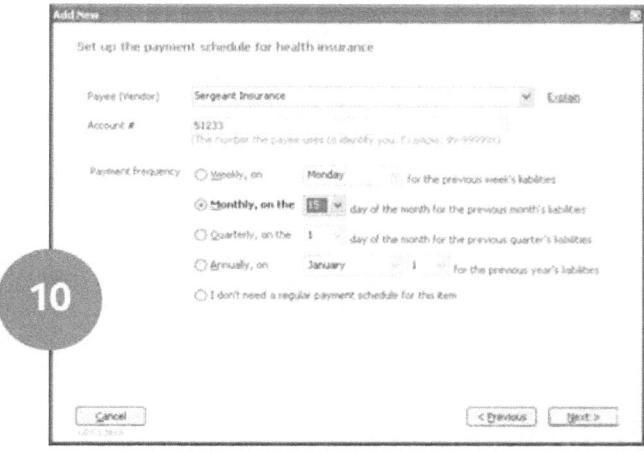

QuickBooks Exercises

How to Create a Customer Statement

Sometimes you want to send statements to customers to remind them of overdue balances, or to list statement charges a customer owes. There are two types of statements in QuickBooks.

The first is called an Open Transaction Statement and the 2nd type is called Activity Based Statement. In this exercise you prepare an Open Transaction Statement and a list of customer's activity over a period of time.

Process an Open Transaction Statement

1. From the Home page, click the Statements icon.
2. In the Select Statement Options section, select a type of statement. Select all open transactions as of Statement Date.
3. Click One Customer.
4. Click the drop-down list and select Brian Cook.
5. Click Preview.
6. Click the mouse to Zoom in.
7. This statement shows only what the customer owes you.
8. Prepare this type of statement if your customer only wants to see outstanding balances without the detail. Click Close.

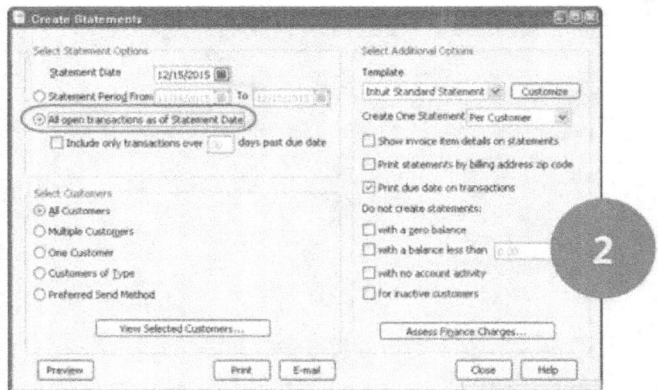

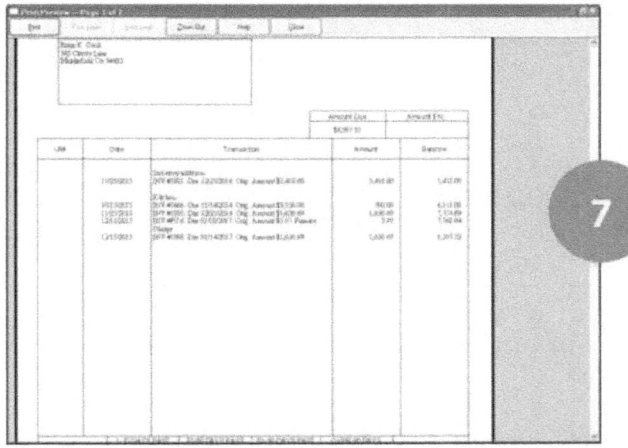

Process a Customer Activity Statement

1. Brian Cook claims he sent a check that wasn't applied to his account. Prepare a statement that shows his activity over a date range. In the Statement Options section, select Statement Period From.

2. Enter a date of November 1st, 2015 to November 30th, 2015.

3. In the Select Customers section, select Brian Cook.

4. Click the Preview button.

5. Click the mouse to Zoom In.

6. An Activity-Based Statement shows all customer account transactions during the time period.

Prepare this type of statement if your customer wants to see the transactions that make up their outstanding balance Click Close.

7. What if Brian Cook reviews his statement but can't find the invoice you sent earlier, so he wants to see the detail of each invoice. Click the box next to Show invoice item details on statements.

8. Click Preview.

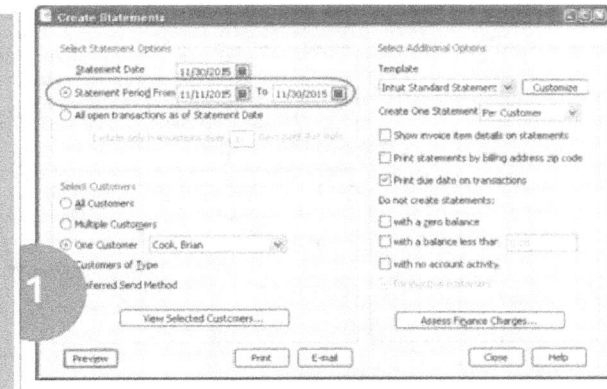

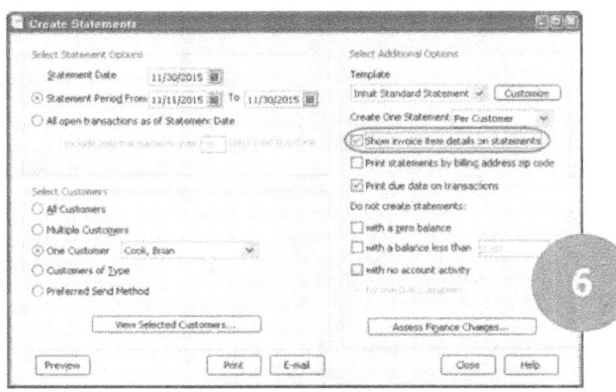

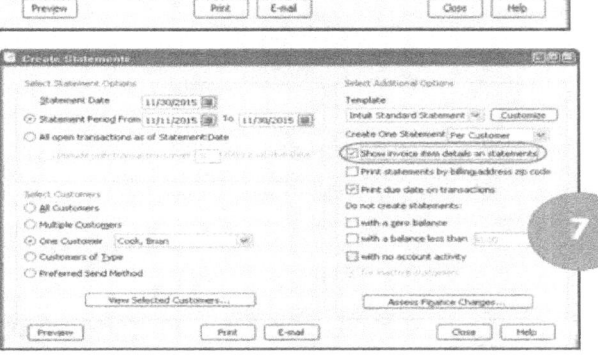

57

How to Merge (Combine) Entries on a List

You'll probably come across this real-world scenario. Someone accidentally enters the same "thing" (name, account, etc.) on a list by accident. This often happens because they misspell the entry. Now you have a problem. The list contains duplicate entries for the same thing. For example, you already had a vendor named "Cal Telephone" and someone else entered a check for "CA Phone". The same vendor is now represented twice in the list. This exercise will show you how to fix that error by merging two entries on the Vendor List (note: this technique works on other lists too with some exceptions - mentioned later).

1. From the Home page, click the Vendor Center.
2. Notice there are 2 names (CA Phone and Cal Telephone). You want to keep Cal Telephone and merge CA Phone and all the associated transactions into Cal Telephone.
3. Type the correct name, Cal Telephone.
4. Click OK.
5. Click Yes to merge the two names.

Now only the correct name, Cal Telephone, appears on the list.

QuickBooks also merged the history (all the transactions) for the two names. That means checks written to both of the vendors are now included in the history for Cal Telephone.

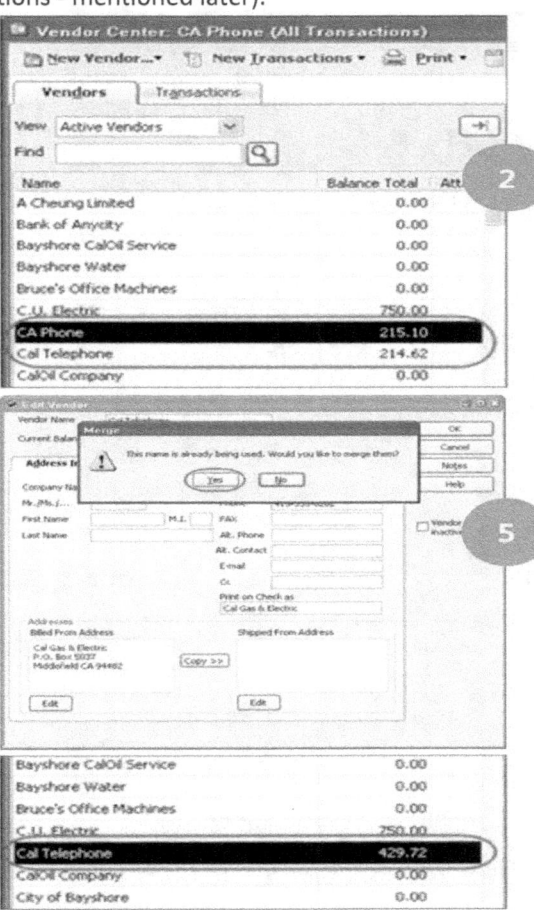

The second restriction only applies to lists with a Type column, like the Chart of Accounts. You can only merge names of the same type. For example, you can merge one expense account with another expense account, but can't merge an expense account with an income account.

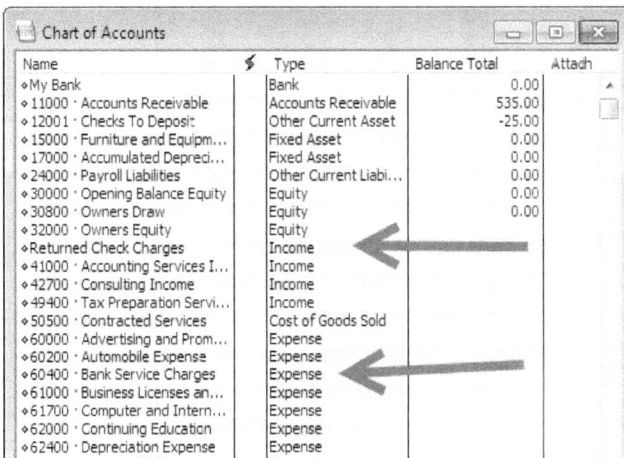

How to Progress Invoice

Sometimes your company might have a job that takes months or even years to finish. Do you wait until the job is finished to start invoicing? In most cases you want to be paid for the work you've completed. This process is called Progress Invoicing. Essentially, you invoice in increments based on an estimate. In this exercise, assume you have already created an estimate for $3,114 for your customer Kristy Abercrombie.

1. First, make sure to turn the progress invoice feature on. To do this click Edit > Preferences and click the Jobs & Estimates icon. Click the Company Preferences tab. In this window select "yes" below "Do you create estimates? And select "yes" below "Do you do progress invoicing?"

2. Prepare an invoice based on the Kristy Abercrombie estimate. Click the Create Invoices icon.

3. Click the Customer: Job drop-down arrow and select the Kristy Abercrombie job.

4. QuickBooks opens the Available Estimates window. Select an estimate to convert it to an invoice. Select estimate number 606.

5. Click OK.

6. QuickBooks opens the Create Progress Invoice Based on Estimate window.

7. Click OK.

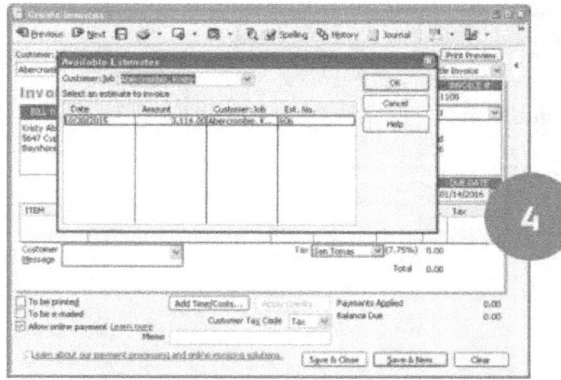

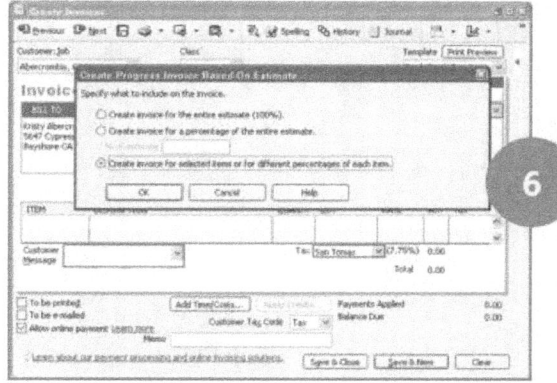

8. Decide which items and quantities to invoice. Click the Show Quantity and Rate and the Show Percentage boxes.

9. The first four columns show information from the Estimate. The next three columns show anything already invoiced for the job. The last six columns show what you want to charge the customer on this invoice.

To transfer an item to the invoice, enter a Quantity, Amount, or Percentage. In this case, enter 3 quantities. For the first line item, enter 5 for Framing.

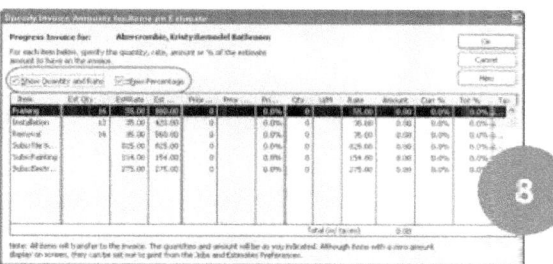

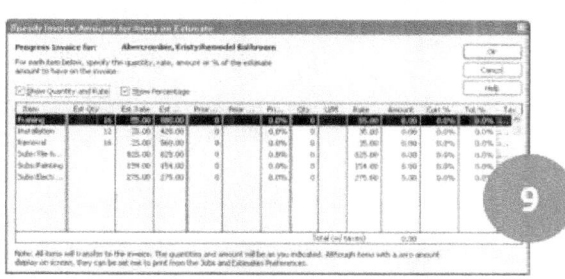

10. For the second line item, enter that you installed 5 Frames.

11. For the third line item, enter that you removed 5 Frames.

12. Click OK.

13. QuickBooks copies the selected items to the invoice.

To print the invoice later, select the To be printed checkbox.

14. Click Save & Close.

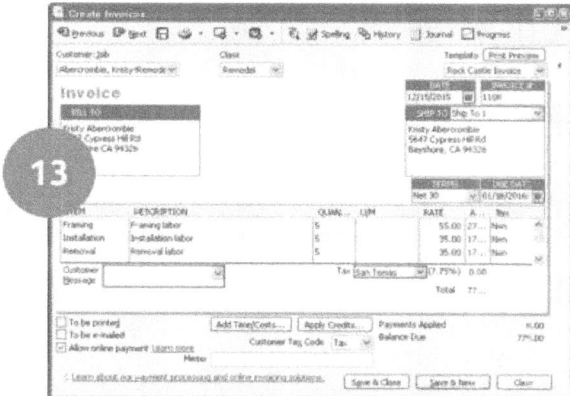

QuickBooks Exercises